FREE AT LAST

A Bibliography of
Martin Luther King, Jr.

by

William H. Fisher

The Scarecrow Press, Inc.
Metuchen, N.J. & London
1977

Library of Congress Cataloging in Publication Data

Fisher, William Harvey, 1950-
    Free at last.

    Includes index.
    1.   King, Martin Luther--Bibliography. 2.   Civil
rights workers--United States--Bibliography.   I.   Title.
Z8464.44.F57   [E185.97.K5]   016.3234'092'4   77-22202
ISBN 0-8108-1081-6

Manufactured in the United States of America

TABLE OF CONTENTS

PREFACE

Perhaps no name is more nearly synonymous with
Black America's struggle for equal rights than that of Martin
Luther King, Jr. In the all too short period of time that he
participated in the civil rights movement, King was personal-
ly involved with some eight major campaigns for racial equality and justice, and supported, in some fashion, a large number of other such campaigns. During the course of his career, King marched hundreds of miles, spoke before count-
less numbers of people, received a variety of awards, med-
als, and prizes including the Nobel Prize for Peace, and still
managed to record his own thoughts on the events in which
he was involved, leaving behind a number of full-length books,
an even larger number of periodical articles, plus the texts
of his many speeches, sermons, letters, and other such material. And, as is the case with people of such prominence,
a large amount of material has been written about Martin
Luther King and his involvement with the civil rights movement.

This bibliography, an attempt to compile the bulk of
the material written by and about Martin Luther King, Jr.,
has been arranged into four sections. The first section,
works written by King, includes material found in manuscript
collections and other unpublished sources, material by King
that can be found reprinted in other sources, as well as the
books and articles he authored. Section II lists books, articles, and other sources of information that are biographical
or in which King is the primary figure. The third section
presents more sources of material about King but in which
he is not the primary focus. Criteria for inclusion in this
section include material that: (1) deals with King more as
a participant than as the central figure in some phase of the
civil rights movement; (2) provides analysis of some second-
ary aspect of his career; (3) presents information about his
relationship with his family, friends, co-workers, and other
figures in the rights struggle; and (4) deals with King's assassination, funeral, the effects of his death, and the search for

and trial of his murderer. Section IV lists reviews of books written by King.

The annotations are provided as a brief guide to enable users to find the material most helpful to them. They are in no way meant to be a detailed description of the contents of a citation. In all instances, the information given tells only how that work relates to King. Citations preceded by an asterisk (*) are considered juvenile literature.

Because of the limitations of time and available resources, many of the non-traditional sources of bibliographic information were not searched for further citations; not included in the bibliography are newspaper articles and foreign language material. Full responsibility for any incorrect citations that have made their way into this bibliography lies with the compiler.

I hope that anyone looking through this bibliography is able to get as much information and enjoyment out of using it as I did in compiling it. May people long continue to study the life and work of Martin Luther King, Jr., for some day his Dream may come true.

William Fisher
February 1977

I

WORKS BY MARTIN LUTHER KING, JR.

MANUSCRIPT COLLECTIONS

Boyle, Sarah P. Papers, University of Virginia Library.
    Material from correspondence with King by this au-
    thor and civil rights leader from Virginia.

Brotherhood of Sleeping Car Porters. Records, 1939-68,
    Library of Congress Manuscript Division.
    Contains correspondence between King and rights
    leader A. Philip Randolph.

"A Comparison of the Conception of God in the Thinking of
    Paul Tillich and Henry Nelson Wieman." Unpublished
    Ph. D. dissertation, Boston University, 1955.
    King's doctoral dissertation.

Hampton Institute. Archives, Hampton Institute Collis P.
    Huntington Memorial Library.
    Some manuscript material by King is available.

King, Martin Luther, Jr. Papers, 1955-61, Boston Univer-
    sity Mugar Memorial Library.
    Material relating to King's early rights drives in-
    cluding the Montgomery boycott and the use of non-vio-
    lent direct action.

_____. Papers and tape recordings, 1950-1968, Martin
    Luther King, Jr. Memorial Center Library Project.
    Material dealing with all aspects of King's life:
    there is material from King's involvement with the SCLC,
    the Montgomery Improvement Association, the Dexter
    Avenue Baptist Church in Montgomery, and other groups
    and rights campaigns.

King, Slater H. Papers, 1959-68, Fisk University Library.
    Correspondence with King by this leader of the rights
    drive in Albany.

1

Martin Luther King Speaks. Tape recordings and other material, SCLC Radio.
Tapes of King's radio broadcasts sponsored by the SCLC.

Project South. Transcripts of tape-recorded interviews, summer, 1965, Stanford University Archives.
Transcript of an address by King recorded by Stanford students representing their student radio station KZSU. The actual recordings are available at Stanford's Library of Recorded Sound.

Saunders, Theodore D. Papers, 1949-67, Chicago Historical Society Library.
Contains a letter by King to Saunders.

Schomburg Collection of Negro Literature and History. Tape recording collection, New York Public Library, 135th Street Branch.
Recordings of some of King's speeches.

Southern Christian Leadership Conference. Files, Southern Christian Leadership Conference.
Correspondence, papers and taped speeches by King.

State Historical Society of Wisconsin. Contemporary Social Action Collection, State Historical Society of Wisconsin.
Contains a taped interview with King.

Wieman, Henry N. Papers, 1927-67, Southern Illinois University Archives.
Includes a letter from King explaining his proposed dissertation topic to Wieman and asking for his support.

MONOGRAPHS

Address at Valedictory Service. Mona, Jamaica: University of the West Indies, 1965.
King addresses a commencement ceremony urging the audience to accept the challenge to develop a world perspective, the challenge to achieve excellence in their various fields of endeavor, and the challenge to overcome racial injustice using non-violent methods.

America's Greatest Crisis. New York: Transport Workers
    Union of America, AFL-CIO, 1961.
    [Not examined.]

Beyond Vietnam. Palo Alto, Calif.: Altoan Press, 1967.
    King's major anti-war statement delivered at New
York's Riverside Church on April 4, 1967.

Conscience for Change. Toronto: Canadian Broadcasting
    Company Publications, 1967.
    Five radio lectures delivered by King for the seventh
annual Massey lectures; they deal with King's philosophy
of non-violence, his anti-war stance, and the need for
vigorous social action.

Declaration of Independence from the War in Vietnam. New
    York: n.p., 1967.
    King's anti-war statement from the Riverside Church
under a different title.

"A Drum Major for Justice." Bushey Heath, Eng.: Taurus
    Press, 1969.
    King delivers his own eulogy in a sermon delivered
at the Ebenezer Baptist Church in Atlanta.

I Have a Dream; The Text of the Speech Delivered August
    28, 1963, at the Lincoln Memorial, Washington, D.C.
    Los Angeles: The John Henry & Mary Louise Dunn Bry-
ant Foundation, 1963.
    The text of King's most popular and oft-quoted work.

Letter from Birmingham City Jail. Philadelphia: American
    Friends Service Committee, 1963.
    Responding to criticism of his activities by eight
Alabama clergymen, King presents his most noted justi-
fication of the civil rights movement and his non-violent
philosophy.

Letter from Birmingham City Jail. Valley Forge: Division
    of Christian Social Concern, 1963.
    Another edition of the above.

A Martin Luther King Treasury. Yonkers, N.Y.: Educa-
    tional Heritage, Inc., 1964.
    Contains King's letter of appeal to President Kennedy
for help in the rights struggle, and versions of Stride
Toward Freedom and Strength to Love.

The Measure of a Man.   Philadelphia: United Church Press,
      1968.
            King presents his philosophical and theological ideas
      on man and how man can lead a more complete life.

Method of Non-Violence.   n. p. , 1957.
            King explains the use of non-violence in the struggle
      against segregation.

Nobel Lecture by the Reverend Dr. Martin Luther King, Jr.,
      Recipient of the 1964 Nobel Peace Prize, Oslo, Norway,
      December 11, 1964.   New York: Harper & Row, Pub-
      lishers, 1965.
            Text of King's acceptance at Nobel ceremonies.

Our Struggle; The Story of Montgomery.   New York: Con-
      gress of Racial Equality, 1957.
            Taken from an article in Liberation in which King
      gives his account of the Montgomery bus boycott.

Sermon, the Washington Cathedral, Sunday, March 31, 1968.
      n. p. , 1968.
            In one of his last major addresses, King speaks of
      America's potential to help eradicate world poverty and
      hunger.

Strength to Love. New York: Harper & Row, Publishers, 1963.
            King deals with "Christian" answers to social prob-
      lems in sermons delivered at the time of the Montgomery
      boycott.

Stride Toward Freedom.   New York: Harper & Row, Pub-
      lishers, 1958.
            King's first book, in which he presents his story of
      the Montgomery boycott and his rationale for the use of
      non-violence.

The Trumpet of Conscience.   New York: Harper & Row,
      Publishers, 1967.
            King's Massey lectures (see Conscience for Change)
      in which he deals with his philosophy of non-violence,
      the war in Vietnam, the role of youth in the world, and
      a hope for world peace.

Where Do We Go from Here: Chaos or Community?   New
      York: Harper & Row, Publishers, 1967.
            King's assessment of the racial situation in which

he discusses "Black Power, " the urban response to the rights movement, and the Meredith march.

Why We Can't Wait. New York: Harper & Row, Publishers, 1963.
    King tells his story of the Birmingham campaign.

Words and Wisdom of Martin Luther King. Bushey Heath, Eng. : Taurus Press, 1970.
    Statements by King dealing with a broad range of subjects.

PERIODICAL ARTICLES

"The Acceptance Speech of Martin Luther King, Jr. of the Nobel Peace Prize on December 10, 1964. " Negro History Bulletin, XXXI (May, 1968), p. 20.
    King's acceptance speech from the Nobel ceremonies.

"Advice for Living. " Ebony, XII (September, 1957), p. 74; XII (October, 1957), p. 53; XIII (December, 1957), p. 120; XIII (January, 1958), p. 34; XIII (February, 1958), p. 84; XIII (March, 1958), p. 92; XIII (April, 1958), p. 104; XIII (May, 1958), p. 112; XIII (July, 1958), p. 86; XIII (August, 1958), p. 78; XIII (September, 1958), p. 68; XIII (October, 1958), p. 138; XIV (November, 1958), p. 138; XIV (December, 1958), p. 159.
    King replies to personal letters dealing with private and public questions directed to him.

"Alabama's Bus Boycott: What It's All About. " U. S. News & World Report, XLI (August 3, 1956), p. 82-89.
    King presents arguments for the boycott, while Grover Hall, editor of the Montgomery Advertiser, presents some objections.

"The American Dream. " Negro History Bulletin, XXXI (May, 1968), p. 10-15.
    King talks of replacing racial myths with reality and the use of non-violence in a 1961 commencement address at Lincoln University.

"America's Racial Crisis. " Current, XCV (May, 1968), p. 6-10.

King presents an economic Bill of Rights as a way
to end poverty.

"Behind the Selma March. " Saturday Review, XLVIII (April
3, 1965), p. 16-17+.
King discusses the goals of the Selma campaign and
the tactics used.

"Beyond Race and Nation. " Current, LXXXVI (May, 1967),
p. 32-40.
King's anti-war statement from his Riverside Church
address.

"Bold Design for a New South. " Nation, CXCVI (March 30,
1963), p. 259-62.
King reviews the events of 1962 and concludes that
Kennedy's administration is still too cautious in dealing
with civil rights.

"Boycotts Will Be Used. " U. S. News & World Report, LVI
(February 24, 1964), p. 59-61.
King discusses the SCLC's plans for rights drives
in 1964.

"The Burning Truth in the South. " Progressive, XXIV (May,
1960), p. 8-10.
King says Southern Negroes can end segregation
using non-violence.

"The Case Against 'Tokenism. '" New York Times Magazine,
August 5, 1962, p. 11+.
King says token integration will not keep the Negro
from seeking full equality and justice.

"Civil Right no. 1--The Right to Vote. " New York Times
Magazine, March 14, 1965, p. 26-27+.
King reaffirms the importance of the franchise in
the Negro's struggle for equality.

"The Civil Rights Struggle in the United States Today. " Rec-
ord of the Association of the Bar of the City of New
York, XX (May, 1965 Supplement), p. 3-24.
King discusses the legal and moral aspects of the
rights movement. This article was reprinted by the
Association XXIII (June, 1968 Supplement), p. 3-19.

"The Current Crisis in Race Relations. " New South, March,

1958, p. 8-12.
King cites resistance to desegregation rulings as a
cause of racial trouble, but he says non-violent reactions
to this resistance will continue.

"Declaration of Independence from the War in Vietnam. "
Ramparts, V (May, 1967), p. 32-37.
A reprint of King's address at the Riverside Church.

"'A Dream ... I Have a Dream. '" Newsweek, LXII (September 9, 1963), p. 21.
Excerpts from King's speech at the Lincoln Memorial.

"'Dreams of Brighter Tomorrows. '" Ebony, XX (March, 1965), p. 34-35.
King's thoughts on receiving the Noble Peace Prize.

"Editorials from Newsletter. " Negro History Bulletin, XXXI
(May, 1968), p. 18.
Two editorials by King from the SCLC Newsletter.

"Equality Now: The President Has the Power. " Nation,
CXCII (February 4, 1961), p. 91-95.
King appeals for strong executive leadership to remove racial barriers to equality.

"The Ethical Demands of Integration. " Religion and Labor
(May, 1963), p. 3.
[Not examined.]

"The Ethics of Love. " Religious Digest, April, 1958, p. 1.
[Not examined.]

"An Experiment in Love. " Jubilee, VI (September, 1958),
p. 11-17.
King discusses the use of non-violence during the
Montgomery boycott.

"Facing the Challenge of a New Age. " Phylon, XVIII (April,
1957), p. 25-34.
King presents challenges in the struggle against
segregation to the first annual Institute on Non-Violence
and Social Change.

"Freedom's Crisis: The Last Steep Ascent. " Nation, CCII
(March 14, 1966), p. 288-92.

As King turns his attention to the conditions in urban ghettos, he calls for a fundamental alteration in the lives of Black Americans.

"From a Birmingham Jail: Excerpts from a Classic Letter. " Jet, XXXIV (April 18, 1968), p. 26-28.
Excerpts from King's famous letter.

"From the Birmingham Jail. " Negro History Bulletin, XXXI (May, 1968), p. 19.
Excerpts from King's famous letter.

"Fumbling on the New Frontier. " Nation, CXCIV (March 3, 1962), p. 190-93.
King calls the efforts of the Kennedy administration in 1961 inadequate and incomplete in civil rights.

"The Future of Integration. " Humanist, XXVIII (March-April, 1968), p. 7-9.
King sees a chance for a true integrated society when Black and White learn that their destinies are linked together.

"A Gift of Love. " McCall's, XCIV (December, 1966), p. 146-47.
King reflects on the suffering some go through in their efforts to speak out in the name of humanity.

"Hammer of Civil Rights. " Nation, CXCVIII (March 9, 1964), p. 230-34.
In reviewing the events of 1963, King cites non-violence as an important factor in achieving gains made that year.

"Hate Is Always Tragic. " Time, LXXX (August 3, 1962), p. 13.
Excerpts from an address by King to the National Press Club.

"Honoring Dr. DuBois. " Freedomways, VIII (Spring, 1968), p. 104-11.
King praises DuBois in a Carnegie Hall speech.

"I Have a Dream. " Negro History Bulletin, XXXI (May, 1968), p. 16-17.
King's speech before the Lincoln Memorial.

"'In a Word--Now.'" New York Times Magazine, September
29, 1963, p. 91-92.
King urges immediate equality for Blacks.

"'It Is Not to Condemn....'" Current, LXXVI (October,
1966), p. 17-19.
King urges a rejection of the "Black Power" movement.

"It's a Difficult Thing to Teach a President." Look, XXVIII
(November 17, 1964), p. 61+.
King's reflections on his dealings with John Kennedy.

"A Legacy of Creative Protest." Massachusetts Review, IV
(Autumn, 1962), p. 43.
King pays tribute to Henry Thoreau.

"'Let Justice Roll Down.'" Nation, CC (March 15, 1965),
p. 169-74.
King cites positive rights gains in his review of the
events of 1964.

"Letter from a Birmingham Jail." Christian Century, LXXX
(June 12, 1963), p. 767-73.

"Letter from a Birmingham Jail." Negro History Bulletin,
XXVII (June, 1964), p. 156.

"Letter from a Birmingham Jail." Time, LXXXIII (January
3, 1964), p. 15.

"Letter from a Birmingham Jail." New Leader, XLVI (June
24, 1963), p. 3-11.

"A Letter from Birmingham Jail." Ebony, XVIII (August,
1963), p. 23-26+.

"Letter from Birmingham Jail." Liberation, VIII (June,
1963), p. 10-16+.

"Letter from the Birmingham City Jail." Interracial Review,
XXXVI (July, 1963), p. 150-55.
The above seven citations contain either the full text
or excerpts from King's letter written while in the Birmingham jail.

"Love, Law and Civil Disobediance." New South, XVI

(December, 1961), p. 3-11.
King discusses the use of non-violence in the student movement of the rights struggle.

"The Luminous Promise." Progressive XXVI (December, 1962), p. 34-37.
King's reflections on the importance and the meaning of the Emancipation Proclamation on that document's 100th anniversary.

"Martin Luther King Defines 'Black Power.'" New York Times Magazine, June 11, 1967, p. 26-27+.
King says Blacks respond to violence because they lack influence on American thought, and he advocates the use of Black economic, political, and ideological power.

"The Most Durable Power." Christian Century, LXXIV (June 5, 1957), p. 708-9.
King urges the rights struggle to be waged with the Christian weapons of love and non-violence.

"My Trip to the Land of Gandhi." Ebony, XIV (July, 1959), p. 84-86+.
King recounts his recent trip to India.

"The Negro Is Your Brother." Atlantic Monthly, CCXII (August, 1963), p. 78-81+.
King's Birmingham letter under a different title.

"Negroes Are Not Moving Too Fast." Saturday Evening Post, CCXXXVII (November 7, 1964), p. 8+.
King seeks more positive action to counter the feeling of frustration on the part of Blacks.

"The 'New Negro' of the South; Behind the Montgomery Story." Socialist Call, June, 1956, p. 16-19.
King provides personal insights into the meaning of the Montgomery boycott.

"A New Sense of Direction." Worldview, XV (April, 1972), p. 5-12.
King reaffirms his faith in non-violence in an address before the SCLC staff shortly before his death.

"Next Stop: The North." Saturday Review, XLVIII (November 13, 1965), p. 33-35+.
King directs the rights campaign to the urban ghettos.

"The Nobel Prize. " Liberation, X (January, 1965), p. 28-29.
King's acceptance speech at the Nobel ceremonies.

"Nonviolence and Racial Justice. " Christian Century, LXXIV
(February 6, 1957), p. 165-67.
King explains how to use non-violence in seeking ra-
cial justice.

"Non-violence: The Only Road to Freedom. " Ebony, XXI
(October, 1966), p. 27-30+.
King recounts the progress made through non-violent
methods and rejects the "Black Power" concept.

"Non-violence, the Only Way. " Indo-Asian Culture, XIII (July,
1964), p. 54-62.
King affirms his faith that non-violence is the way to
deal with the race problem.

"On Nonviolent Resistance. " Religion in Life, XXVI (Summer,
1957), p. 335-44.
King explains his philosophy of non-violence.

"Our Struggle. " Liberation, I (April, 1956), p. 3-6.
King discusses the Montgomery boycott.

"Out of Segregation's Long Night; An Interpretation of a Racial Crisis. " Churchman, CLXXII (February, 1958),
p. 7.
King urges the use of non-violence to combat Southern
resistance to desegregation rulings.

"Out of the Long Night of Segregation. " Advance, CL (February 28, 1958), p. 14-15+.
King discusses the forces creating the racial crisis
in America and presents his views on how non-violence
can be used to secure racial equality and justice.

"Pilgrimage to Nonviolence. " Christian Century, LXXVII
(April 13, 1960), p. 439-41.
King recounts the development of his philosophy of
non-violence.

"Playboy Interview with Martin Luther King. " Playboy XII
(January, 1965), p. 65-68+.
King discusses his rise to prominence, the current
status of the rights movement, and other topics.

"The Power of Nonviolence. " Intercollegian, LXXV (May, 1958), p. 8-9.
    King discusses the philosophical justification of non-violence before a crowd at Berkeley.

"Rev. Dr. Martin Luther King's 'I Have a Dream. '" Jet, XXXIV (April 18, 1968), p. 34-35.
    Text of King's speech before the Lincoln Memorial.

"Revolt Without Violence--The Negroes' New Strategy. " U. S. News & World Report, XLVIII (March 21, 1960), p. 76-8.
    King discusses the uses of non-violence in the rights struggle.

"The Rising Tide of Racial Consciousness. " YWCA Magazine, December, 1960, p. 4-6.
    King says the Negro must take primary responsibility in achieving first-class citizenship.

"Role of the Behaviorial Scientist in the Civil Rights Movement. " Journal of Social Issues, XXIV (January, 1968), p. 1-12.
    King sees a need for social scientists to examine the problem of Negro leadership, Black political action, and psychological and ideological changes in the Negro.

"'Say That I Was a Drum Major. '" Reader's Digest, XCII (June, 1968), p. 58-59.
    King delivers his own eulogy in a sermon at the Ebenezer Baptist Church in Atlanta.

"Selma--The Shame and the Promise. " I. U. D. Agenda, I (March, 1965), p. 18-21.
    King discusses the issues in the Selma campaign.

"Showdown for Non-violence. " Look, XXXII (April 16, 1968), p. 23-25.
    King feels that non-violence can dominate the rights movement and discusses plans for Poor People's march.

"The Social Organization of Nonviolence. " Liberation, III (October, 1959), p. 5-6.
    King discusses the use of non-violence to counter against token integration.

"Suffering and Faith. " Christian Century, LXXVII (April 27, 1960), p. 510.

King reflects upon his personal trials.

"Tears of Love; A Letter From His Birmingham Jail Cell. "
Progressive, XXVII (July, 1963), p. 9-13.
King's Birmingham letter.

"A Testament of Hope. " Playboy, XVI (January, 1969), p.
175+.
King reflects upon the current situation in America
and sees the promise of a better tomorrow.

"'The Time for Freedom Has Come. '" New York Times
Magazine, September 10, 1961, p. 25+.
King discusses the new awareness and vigor in the
struggle for equality.

"A Time to Break Silence. " Freedomways, VII (Spring, 1967),
p. 103-17.
King's anti-war speech from the Riverside Church.

"The Un-Christian Christian. " Ebony, XX (August, 1965), p.
76-80.
King speaks of people who follow Christianity emo-
tionally, but not morally.

"A View from the Mountaintop; Dr. King's Last Message. "
Renewal, IX (April, 1969), p. 3-5.
Excerpts from King's last speech delivered in Mem-
phis the day before his death.

"A View of the Dawn. " Interracial Review, May, 1957, p.
82-85.
King feels the Negro position of second-class citizen
must be removed before advancement toward racial equality can be made.

"Walk for Freedom. " Fellowship, XXII (May, 1956), p. 5-7.
King discusses the Montgomery boycott and the use of
non-violence.

"We Are Still Walking. " Liberation, I (December, 1956), p.
6-9.
King explains the situation in Montgomery.

"We Shall Overcome. " I. U. D. Digest, VII (Spring, 1962), p.
19-27.
King draws a parallel between the rights and labor

movements and speaks of their similar goals.

"White Editor, Rev. King Debate Sit-in Strikes." Jet, XIX
(December 8, 1960), p. 6-7.
King supports the use of sit-ins, while James J. Kil-
patrick says they can't be justified.

"'Who Is Their God?'" Nation, CXCV (October 13, 1962),
p. 209-10.
King comments on the situation in Mississippi as
James Meredith integrates the University of Mississippi.

"Who Speaks for the South?" Liberation, II (March, 1958),
p. 13-14.
King says the South is not truly represented because
the Negroes' franchise is restricted.

"Why the Negro Won't Wait." Financial Post, LVII (July 27,
1963), p. 6.
King says Negroes are tired of waiting for the moderates to decide that justice must come before order.

MATERIAL REPRINTED in OTHER SOURCES

MONOGRAPHS/ANTHOLOGIES

Adoff, Arnold, comp. Black on Black; Commentaries by
Black Americans. New York: Macmillan Company,
1968.
King's Birmingham letter.

Ahmann, Mathew, ed. Race: Challenge to Religion. Chicago: Henry Regnery Company, 1963.
King says the Christian ethics must make a stand
against injustice in "A Challenge to the Churches and
Synagogues."

Ames, William C. The Negro Struggle for Equality in the
Twentieth Century. Boston: D. C. Heath & Company,
1965.
Excerpts from Kenneth Clark's interview with King
and excerpts from the Birmingham letter.

Andrews, James R. , comp. A Choice of Words; The Practice and Criticism of Public Discourse. New York: Harper & Row Publishers, 1973).
  King's "I Have a Dream" speech.

Baker, Ross K. , ed. The Afro-American. New York: Van Nostrand-Reinhold Company, 1970.
  Excerpt on "Black Power" from Where Do We Go from Here?

Bell, Derrick A. Race, Racism, and American Law. Boston: Little, Brown and Company, 1973.
  King's Birmingham letter.

Blaustein, Albert P. , and Robert L. Zangrando, eds. Civil Rights and the Black American: A Documentary History. New York: Simon & Schuster, Inc. , 1968.
  King's Birmingham letter.

Bosmajian, Haig A. , ed. Readings in Speech. 2nd ed. New York: Harper & Row Publishers, Inc. , 1971.
  King's anti-war address, "Beyond Vietnam. "

_____, and Hamida Bosmajian, comps. The Rhetoric of the Civil Rights Movement. New York: Random House, 1969.
  King's Birmingham letter.

Boulware, Marcus H. The Oratory of Negro Leaders: 1900-1968. Westport, Conn. : Negro Universities Press, 1969.
  King's "I Have a Dream" speech and "Love, Law, and Civil Disobedience. "

Bracey, John H. , Jr. , August Meier, and Elliott Rudwick, eds. The Afro-Americans: Selected Documents. Boston: Allyn and Bacon, Inc. , 1972.
  Excerpts from "Our Struggle" and "Walk for Freedom" giving King's views on the Montgomery boycott.

Branson, Margaret S. , and Edward E. France, eds. The Human Side of Afro-American History. Lexington, Mass.: Ginn and Company, 1972.
  Excerpts from Stride Toward Freedom.

Broderick, Francis L. , and August Meier, eds. Negro Protest Thought in the Twentieth Century. Indianapolis: Bobbs-Merrill Company, Inc. , 1965.

Excerpts from Stride Toward Freedom and the "I Have a Dream" speech.

Burnett, Hugh, ed. Face to Face. New York: Stein & Day Publishers, 1965.
    Excerpts from King's interview on "Face to Face."

Chambers, Bradford, ed. Chronicles of Negro Protest. New York: Parents' Magazine Press, 1968.
    Excerpts from Stride Toward Freedom.

Clayton, Edward T. The Negro Politician; His Success and Failure. Chicago: Johnson Publishing Company, Inc., 1964.
    Contains an introduction by King.

Commager, Henry S., ed. The Struggle for Racial Equality: A Documentary Record. New York: Harper & Row Publishers, 1967.
    Excerpts from Stride Toward Freedom and the Birmingham letter.

Cuban, Larry. The Negro in America. Chicago: Scott Foresman and Company, 1964.
    Excerpts from Stride Toward Freedom.

Daniel, Bradford, ed. Black, White and Gray; Twenty-one Points of View on the Race Question. New York: Sheed and Ward, 1964.
    King's Birmingham letter.

David, Jay, and Elaine Crane, eds. Living Black in White America. New York: William Morrow and Company, Inc., 1971.
    Excerpts from Stride Toward Freedom.

Estey, George F., and Doris A. Hunter, eds. Nonviolence; A Reader in the Ethics of Action. Waltham, Mass.: Xerox College Publishing, 1971.
    King's Birmingham letter.

Ezekiel, Nissim, ed. A Martin Luther King Reader. Bombay: Popular Prakashan, 1969.
    Excerpts from many of King's speeches, sermons, and writings.

Fey, Harold E., and Margaret Frakes. The Christian Cen-

tury Reader. New York: Association Press, 1962.
"Non-violence and Racial Justice" from Christian Century, February 1957.

Fishel, Leslie H., Jr., and Benjamin Quarles, eds. The Black American; A Documentary History. New York: William Morrow and Company, Inc., 1970.
The Birmingham letter and "I Have a Dream" speech.

Foner, Philip S. The Voice of Black America; Major Speeches by Negroes in the United States, 1797-1971. New York: Simon & Schuster, 1972.
"I Have a Dream," "I See the Promised Land," and other speeches.

_____, ed. W. E. B. DuBois Speaks; Speeches and Addresses, 1890-1919. New York: Pathfinder Press, 1970.
Contains King's speech "Honoring Dr. DuBois."

Franklin, John H., and Isidore Starr, eds. Negro in Twentieth Century America: A Reader on the Struggle for Civil Rights. New York: Vintage Books, 1967.
The Birmingham letter and "I Have a Dream" speech.

Friedman, Leon, ed. The Civil Rights Reader; Basic Documents of the Civil Rights Movement. New York: Walker & Company, 1967.
Excerpts from Stride Toward Freedom and "I Have a Dream."

Gayle, Addison, Jr., ed. Bondage Freedom and Beyond: The Prose of Black Americans. Garden City, N.Y.: Doubleday & Company, Inc., 1971.
King's "Yes, We Shall Overcome," in which he says all men need to learn how to live together in universal brotherhood.

Girvetz, Harry K., ed. Contemporary Moral Issues. Belmont, Calif.: Wadsworth Publishing Company, 1963.
Excerpts from Stride Toward Freedom.

Golden, James L., and Richard D. Rieke, The Rhetoric of Black Americans. Columbus: Charles E. Merrill Publishing Company, 1971.
Excerpts from "Facing the Challenge of a New Age" and "I Have a Dream" speech.

Goldwin, Robert A. , ed.   On Civil Disobedience; American
    Essays, Old and New.   Chicago: Rand McNally & Com-
    pany, 1970.
        King's Birmingham letter.

Goodman, Paul. Seeds of Liberation. New York: George
    Braziller, Inc. , 1964.
        King's "Our Struggle" and "The Social Organization
    of Nonviolence" from Liberation.

Grant, Joanne, ed. Black Protest: History, Documents, and
    Analyses 1619 to the Present.   New York: St. Martin's
    Press, 1970.
        Excerpts from Stride Toward Freedom and King's
    anti-war speech at the Riverside Church.

Gregg, Richard B.   The Power of Nonviolence, 2nd rev. ed.
    New York: Fellowship Publications.
        Contains a foreword by King.

Gregory, Richard C.   No More Lies: The Myth and the
    Reality of American History. New York: Harper & Row
    Publishers, 1971.
        Excerpts from King's speech, "A View from the
    Mountaintop. "

Haberman, Frederick W. , ed.   Nobel Lectures--Peace, 1951-
    1970. Vol. 3. New York: Elsevier Publishing Company,
    1972.
        King's Nobel acceptance speech, "The Quest for
    Peace and Justice. "

Hale, Frank W. , Jr. , ed. The Cry for Freedom: An An-
    thology of the Best That Has Been Said and Written on
    Civil Rights Since 1954. New York: A. S. Barnes and
    Company, 1969.
        The Birmingham letter, "I Have a Dream" and King's
    Nobel acceptance speech.

Hamilton, Michael P. , ed.   The Vietnam War: Christian
    Perspectives. Grand Rapids, Mich. : William B. Eerd-
    mans Publishing Company, 1967.
        King's anti-war address from the Riverside Church.

Hare, A. Paul, and Herbert H. Blumberg, eds. Nonviolent
    Direct Action; American Cases: Social-Psychological
    Analyses. Washington: Corpus Books, 1968.
        Excerpts from Stride Toward Freedom.

*Harrison, Deloris, ed. We Shall Live in Peace: The Teachings of Martin Luther King, Jr. New York: Hawthorn Books, Inc. , 1968.
Excerpts from King's speeches and writings.

Heinz, H. John, III, ed. Crisis in Modern America: A Series of Lectures on Two Areas of Conflict in Our Society: Civil Rights and Economic Life. New Haven, Conn. : Yale University, 1959.
Text of King's address at Yale.

Hill, Roy L. , ed. Rhetoric of Racial Revolt. Denver: Golden Bell Press, 1964.
"I Have a Dream" and "Love, Law, and Civil Disobedience. "

Hoskins, Lottie, ed. "I Have a Dream": The Quotations of Martin Luther King, Jr. New York: Grosset & Dunlap, 1968.
Statements by King on a wide range of topics.

Hoyt, Robert G. Martin Luther King, Jr. Waukesha, Wisc. : Country Beautiful Foundation, Inc. , 1970.
Excerpts from King's speeches and writings.

Huie, William B. Three Lives for Mississippi. New York: New American Library, 1968.
Contains an introduction by King.

Ianniello, Lynne, ed. Milestones Along the March; Twelve Historic Civil Rights Documents--From World War II to Selma. New York: Fredrick A. Praeger Publishers, 1965.
King's Birmingham letter.

Kunstler, William M. Deep in My Heart. New York: William Morrow & Company, 1966.
Contains a foreword by King.

Lincoln, C. Eric, ed. Is Anybody Listening to Black America? New York: Seabury Press, 1968.
Excerpts from Where Do We Go from Here?, the "I Have a Dream" speech, and the "Drum Major for Justice" sermon.

Linkugel, Wil A. , R. R. Allen, and Richard L. Johannesen, eds. Contemporary American Speeches; A Sourcebook of

Speech Forms and Principles. Belmont, Calif.: Wadsworth Publishing Company, Inc., 1965.
"I Have a Dream" and "Love, Law, and Civil Disobedience."

Littleton, Arthur C., and Mary W. Burger, eds. Black Viewpoints. New York: New American Library, Inc., 1971.
Excerpts from the Birmingham letter and the Look article, "Showdown for Non-violence."

Long, Richard A., and Eugenia W. Collier, eds. Afro-American Writing; An Anthology of Prose and Poetry. Vol. II. New York: New York University Press, 1972.
Contains "Facing the Challenge of a New Age."

Lynd, Staughton, ed. Nonviolence in America: A Documentary History. Indianapolis: Bobbs-Merrill Company, Inc., 1966.
Excerpts from Stride Toward Freedom and the Birmingham letter.

McClellan, Grant S., ed. Civil Rights. New York: H.W. Wilson Company, 1964.
Excerpt from Why We Can't Wait.

Marx, Gary T. Racial Conflict; Tension and Change in American Society. Boston: Little, Brown and Company, 1971.
Excerpts from Stride Toward Freedom.

Mayer, Peter, ed. The Pacifist Conscience. New York: Holt, Rinehart and Winston, 1966.
Contains King's "Pilgrimage to Nonviolence" and "Suffering and Faith."

Meier, August, Elliott Rudwick, and Francis L. Broderick, eds. Black Protest Thought in the Twentieth Century, 2nd ed. Indianapolis: Bobbs-Merrill Company, Inc., 1971.
Excerpts from Stride Toward Freedom, "I Have a Dream" and "Showdown for Nonviolence."

Messner, Gerald, ed. Another View: To Be Black in America. New York: Harcourt, Brace & World, Inc., 1970.
Contains King's Playboy article, "A Testament of Hope."

Moss, James A. , ed. The Black Man in America; Integration and Separation. New York: Delta Books, 1971.
  Contains the Humanist article, "Future of Integration. "

The Negro in American History. Vol. I. Chicago: Encyclopaedia Britannica Educational Corporation, 1969.
  The Birmingham letter, "I Have a Dream" and "Showdown for Nonviolence. "

Nelsen, Hart M. , Raythea L. Yokley, and Annek Nelsen. The Black Church in America. New York: Basic Books, Inc. , 1971.
  King's Birmingham letter.

Osofsky, Gilbert. Burden of Race: A Documentary History of Negro-White Relations in America. New York: Harper & Row Publishers, 1967.
  Excerpts from King's writings on non-violence.

Rose, Peter I. , ed. Old Memories, New Moods. New York: Atherton Press, Inc. , 1970.
  Excerpts from Where Do We Go from Here?

Saunders, Doris E. , ed. The Day They Marched. Chicago: Johnson Publishing Company, Inc. , 1963.
  King's "I Have a Dream" speech.

Scott, Robert L. and Wayne Brockriede, comps. The Rhetoric of Black Power. New York: Harper & Row, Publishers, 1969.
  Excerpts from Where Do We Go from Here?

Sibley, Mulford Q. The Quiet Battle: Writings on the Theory and Practice of Non-Violent Resistance. Boston: Beacon Press, 1963.
  Contains the article "The Time for Freedom Has Come. "

Smith, Arthur L. and Stephen Robb. The Voice of Black Rhetoric: Selections. Boston: Allyn and Bacon, Inc. , 1971.
  Contains "I Have a Dream, " "A Long Way to Go" and "Honoring Dr. DuBois."

Thonssen, Lester, ed. Representative American Speeches, 1963-1964. New York: H. W. Wilson Company, 1964.
  King's "I Have a Dream" speech.

Twombly, Robert C. , ed. Blacks in White America Since
1865; Issues and Interpretations. New York: David Mc-
Kay Company, Inc. , 1971.
    Excerpts from Stride Toward Freedom and "I Have
a Dream. "

Wade, Richard C. , ed. The Negro in American Life; Selected Readings. Boston: Houghton Mifflin Company,
1965.
    Excerpts from Stride Toward Freedom and "I Have
a Dream. "

Warren, Robert P. Who Speaks for the Negro? New York:
Random House, 1965.
    Excerpts from an interview with King.

Weinberg, Arthur, and Lila Weinberg, eds. Instead of Violence; Writings by the Great Advocates of Peace and Non-
violence Throughout History. New York: Grossman Publishers, 1963.
    Contains King's "Pilgrimage to Nonviolence. "

Westin, Alan F. , ed. Freedom Now! The Civil Rights
Struggle in America. New York: Basic Books, Inc. ,
1964.
    King's Birmingham letter.

The White Problem in America. Chicago: Johnson Publishing Company, Inc. , 1966.
    Contains King's article "The Un-Christian Christian. "

Williams, Robert F. Negroes with Guns. New York: Mar-
zani & Munsell, Inc. , 1962.
    Contains King's "The Social Organization of Non-
violence" and "Hate Is Always Tragic. "

Wish, Harvey, ed. The Negro Since Emancipation. Englewood Cliffs: Prentice-Hall, Inc. , 1964.
    Excerpts from Stride Toward Freedom.

Young, Richard P. , ed. Roots of Rebellion; The Evolution
of Black Politics and Protest Since World War II. New
York: Harper & Row Publishers, 1970.
    King's Birmingham letter.

PERIODICAL ARTICLES

"The Church and the Race Crisis. " Christian Century, LXXV
(October 8, 1958), p. 1140-41.
Excerpts from Stride Toward Freedom.

"Dark Yesterdays, Bright Tomorrows. " Reader's Digest,
XCII (June, 1968), p. 55-58.
Excerpts from Strength to Love.

"Dr. King: In Tribute. " Christian Century, LXXXV (April
17, 1968), p. 503.
Excerpts from prior Christian Century articles by
King.

"Emancipation--1963. " Renewal, III (June, 1963), p. 2-3.
Excerpts from King's Birmingham letter.

"The Living Legacy of Martin Luther King, Jr. " Senior
Scholastic, XCII (April 25, 1968), p. 19.
Excerpts from statements made by King on various
subjects.

"Love and Nonviolence and the Shame of Segregation. " Jubilee, XI (July, 1963), p. 22-23.
Excerpts from Strength to Love.

"M. L. King. " Catholic Worker, XXX (October, 1963), p. 7.
Excerpts from Strength to Love.

"The Man Who Was a Fool. " Sepia, X (February, 1962), p.
31-33.
Excerpts from Strength to Love.

"Speeches by Dr. Martin Luther King, Jr. " Negro History
Bulletin, XXXI (May, 1968), p. 22-23.
Excerpts from some of King's speeches.

"The Sword That Heals; Excerpts from Why We Can't Wait. "
Critic, XXII (June-July, 1964), p. 6-14.
Excerpts from Why We Can't Wait.

"Visions of the Promised Land. " Time, XCI (April 12,
1968), p. 20.
Some of King's more famous quotes.

"Why We Can't Wait. " Life, LVI (May 15, 1964), p. 98-
100+.
Excerpts from the book.

"Why We Can't Wait. " Saturday Review, XLVII (May 30,
1964), p. 17-20.
Excerpts from the book.

"The Words of Martin Luther King, Jr. , Can Live On in the
Minds of Our Children. " Instructor, LXXVII (June,
1968), p. 17.
Excerpts from Strength to Love.

CONGRESSIONAL RECORD
(In Chronological Order)

United States. Congress. Senate. 85th Cong. , 1st sess. ,
May 28, 1957. Congressional Record, CIII, 7822-24.
King's "Prayer Pilgrimage for Freedom" speech,
delivered at the Lincoln Memorial on May 17, 1957.

_____. _____. House. 86th Cong. , 1st sess. , May 20, 1959.
Congressional Record, CV, 8696-97.
King's speech before the Youth March for Integrated
Schools.

_____. _____. _____. 87th Cong. , 1st sess. , May 2, 1961.
Congressional Record, CVII, A3007-9.
King's article, "Equality Now, " taken from the Feb-
ruary, 1961, Nation.

_____. _____. Senate. 87th Cong. , 2nd sess. , July 20, 1962.
Congressional Record, CVIII, 14247-49.
The text of King's address to the National Press Club.

_____. _____. House. 88th Cong. , 1st sess. , July 11, 1963.
Congressional Record, CIX, A4366-68.

_____. _____. _____. 88th Cong. , 1st sess. , July 15, 1963.
Congressional Record, CIX, A4409-13.

_____. _____. _____. 88th Cong. , 1st sess. , July 15, 1963.
Congressional Record, CIX, A4414-18.

———. ———. ———. 88th Cong., 1st sess., July 15, 1963. Congressional Record, CIX, A4418-20.

   The above four citations are all for reprints of King's Birmingham letter.

———. ———. ———. 88th Cong., 1st sess., September 3, 1963. Congressional Record, CIX, A5590-91. King's "I Have a Dream" speech.

———. ———. Senate. 88th Cong., 2nd sess., May 16, 1964. Congressional Record, CX, 11070.
   Text of King's speech before the March on Washington for Jobs and Freedom.

———. ———. House. 89th Cong., 1st sess., March 15, 1965. Congressional Record, CXI, A1176-78.
   King's article, "Civil Right no. 1--The Right to Vote," from the New York Times Magazine.

———. ———. ———. 89th Cong., 2nd sess., August 25, 1966. Congressional Record, CXII, A4516-17.
   King's article, "It Is Not Enough to Condemn Black Power," from the New York Times Magazine.

———. ———. Senate. 89th Cong., 2nd sess., August 29, 1966. Congressional Record, CXII, 21095-102.
   Transcript of a "Meet the Press" show on which King appeared.

———. ———. House. 90th Cong., 1st sess., May 2, 1967. Congressional Record, CXIII, 11402-5.
   King's anti-war speech from the Riverside Church.

———. ———. Senate. 90th Cong., 1st sess., May 18, 1967. Congressional Record, CXIII, 13222-25.
   King's anti-war speech from the Riverside Church.

———. ———. ———. 90th Cong., 1st sess., July 12, 1967. Congressional Record, CXIII, 18515-16.
   A letter to Sen. Philip Hart from King and Albert Raby protesting about employment opportunities at a proposed Atomic Energy Commission facility.

———. ———. ———. 90th Cong., 1st sess., August 9, 1967. Congressional Record, CXIII, 22055-59.
   Transcript of a "Face to Face" show on which King appeared.

———.   .   .   90th Cong., 2nd sess., April 5, 1968.
Congressional Record, CXIV, 9143-45.
King's "Showdown for Nonviolence" from Look.

———.   .   House.   90th Cong., 2nd sess., April 8, 1968.
Congressional Record, CXIV, 9164-65. (Also on p. 9267-68.)
King's "I Have a Dream" speech.

———.   .   .   90th Cong., 2nd sess., April 9, 1968.
Congressional Record, CXIV, 9391-97.
King's "Beyond Vietnam" from the Riverside Church and "Remaining Awake Through a Great Revolution," a sermon he delivered at the Washington National Cathedral.

———.   .   Senate.   91st Cong., 1st sess., January 15, 1969.   Congressional Record, CXV, 866-67.

———.   .   .   91st Cong., 2nd sess., March 13, 1970.
Congressional Record, CXVI, 7338-39.

———.   .   .   93rd Cong., 1st sess., September 5, 1973.   Congressional Record, CXIX, 28522-23.
The above three citations all refer to reprints of King's "I Have a Dream" speech.

II

WORKS SPECIFICALLY ON KING

MONOGRAPHS

Alexander, Mithrapuram K. Martin Luther King--Martyr for
Freedom. New Delhi: New Light Publishers, 1968.
    Biographical treatment of King from his childhood
through his death.

Baldwin, James, et al. The Negro Protest; James Baldwin,
Malcolm X, & Martin Luther King Talk with Kenneth
B. Clark. Boston: Beacon Press, 1963.
    King comments about his life, family, philosophy of
non-violence, and the status of the rights movement.

Bales, James D. "The Martin Luther King Story." Tulsa:
Christian Crusade Publications, 1967.
    An attempt to link King to Communism, supported
by a number of statements by King, most of which are
taken out of context.

Bennett, Lerone, Jr. What Manner of Man: A Biography
of Martin Luther King, Jr. Chicago: Johnson Publishing Company, Inc., 1964.
    An early biography of King's life through his recep-
tion of the Nobel Peace Prize; good treatment of his
early life and the influences upon him that helped develop
his character and thinking.

Bishop, Jim. The Days of Martin Luther King, Jr. New
York: G. P. Putnam's Sons, 1971.
    Coverage of King's career and the events surround-
ing his assassination.

Bleiweiss, Robert M., ed. Marching to Freedom: The Life
of Martin Luther King, Jr. New York: New American
Library, 1968.
    Coverage of King's childhood, major rights cam-
paigns, and his assassination.

27

*Boone-Jones, Margaret. <u>Martin Luther King, Jr.; A Picture Story</u>. Chicago: Childrens Press, 1968.
General treatment of King's life.

*Clayton, Ed. <u>Martin Luther King: The Peaceful Warrior</u>, 3rd ed. Englewood Cliffs, N. J.: Prentice-Hall, 1970.
This biography has a good treatment of King's childhood, education, and marriage.

Clemens, Thomas C. <u>Martin Luther King, Man of Peace</u>. Washington, D. C.: U. S. Information Service, 1965.
[Not examined.]

Davis, Lenwood G. <u>I Have a Dream: The Life and Times of Martin Luther King, Jr</u>. Westport, Conn.: Negro Universities Press, 1969.
Analysis of the influences of King's education upon his thinking, and accounts of his major campaigns in the struggle for equality.

*"Dear Dr. King ...": <u>A Tribute in Words and Pictures by the Children of the Richard J. Bailey School</u>. Jamaica, N. Y.: Buckingham Enterprises, Inc., 1968.
A memorial to King prepared by some New York school children.

*de Kay, James T. <u>Meet Martin Luther King, Jr</u>. New York: Random House, 1969.
This juvenile biography has good coverage of the major aspects of King's life as a civil rights leader.

Feuerlicht, Roberta S. <u>Martin Luther King, Jr.; A Concise Biography</u>. New York: American R. D. M. Corporation, 1966.
King's career from Montgomery through the Selma march is covered in this biography.

Frank, Gerold. <u>An American Death: The True Story of the Assassination of Dr. Martin Luther King, Jr. and the Greatest Manhunt of Our Time</u>. Garden City, N. Y.: Doubleday & Company, Inc., 1972.
An account of King's assassination, the search for and capture of James Earl Ray, and his trial.

George, Emery E. <u>Black Jesus</u>. Ann Arbor, Mich.: Kylix Press, 1974.
A poetic tribute to King.

I Have a Dream; The Story of Martin Luther King in Text and
　　Pictures. New York: Time-Life Books, 1968.
　　　　Pictorial biography of King.

King, Coretta S. My Life with Martin Luther King, Jr. New
　　York: Holt, Rinehart, and Winston, 1969.
　　　　Coretta King's life with Martin from their marriage
　　in 1953 until his death.

Lewis, David L. King; A Critical Biography. New York:
　　Fredrick A. Praeger Publishers, 1970.
　　　　Analysis of King's major rights drives and their suc-
　　cess or failure.

Lincoln, C. Eric, ed. Martin Luther King, Jr.; A Profile.
　　New York: Hill & Wang, 1970.
　　　　An anthology of biographical works on King by Lerone
　　Bennett, L. D. Reddick, August Meier, Ralph Abernathy,
　　and others.

Lokos, Lionel. House Divided; The Life and Legacy of Mar-
　　tin Luther King. New York: Arlington House, 1968.
　　　　Analysis of King's major rights campaigns, which
　　the author sees as becoming more dependent upon left-
　　wing support.

Lomax, Louis E. To Kill a Black Man. Los Angeles: Hol-
　　loway House Publishing Co., 1968.
　　　　A comparison of the lives of King and Malcolm X.

Lyght, Ernest S. Religious and Philosophical Foundations in
　　the Thought of Martin Luther King. New York: Vantage
　　Press, 1972.
　　　　[Not examined.]

*McKee, Don. Martin Luther King. New York: G. P. Put-
　　nam's Sons, 1969.
　　　　[Not examined.]

Martin Luther King, Jr.; His Three-Pronged Attack on: I.
　　Christ and the Bible, II. The United States of America,
　　III. Law and Order. Wheaton, Ill.: Church League of
　　America, 1968.
　　　　Right-wing attack on King trying to link him to Com-
　　munism.

Martin Luther King, Jr.: Man and Teacher. Baltimore:

Vinmar Lithographing Company, 1968.
Pictorial biography in tribute to King.

Martin Luther King, Jr., The Journey of a Martyr.   New
York: Award Books, 1968.
[Not examined.]

Martin Luther King, 1929-1968.   Chicago: Johnson Publishing Co., 1968.
Pictorial biography of King prepared by the editorial
staff of Ebony.

Matthews, Jim.   Five Dark Days in History.   Los Angeles:
Creative Advertising Media, 1968.
Biographical material on King with an emphasis upon
his assassination and funeral.

*Merriam, Eve.   I Am a Man: Ode to Martin Luther King,
Jr.   Garden City, N.Y.:   Doubleday & Company, Inc.,
1971.
General biographical treatment of King's life.

*Millender, Dharathula.   Martin Luther King, Jr.:   Boy with
a Dream.   Indianapolis: Bobbs-Merrill Company, Inc.,
1969.
[Not examined.]

Miller, William R.   Martin Luther King, Jr.; His Life,
Martyrdom and Meaning for the World.   New York: Wey-
bright & Talley, Inc., 1968.
Biographical treatment of King and his major rights
drives, with an analysis of the development and use of
King's philosophy of non-violence.

*Muller, Gerald F.   Martin Luther King, Jr.; Civil Rights
Leader.   Minneapolis: T.S. Denison and Company, Inc.,
1970.
King's life from his childhood in Atlanta to his assassination.

*Patterson, Lillie.   Martin Luther King, Jr.; Man of Peace.
Champaign, Ill.:   Garrard Publishing Co., 1969.
Good coverage of King's early life and his career
through his reception of the Nobel Peace Prize.

*Peck, Ira.   The Life and Words of Martin Luther King, Jr.
New York: Scholastic Book Services, 1968.

Biography of King covering the major aspects of his life.

Pillai, Vijay, comp. Indian Leaders on Martin Luther King, Jr. New Delhi: Inter-state Cultural League of India, 1968.
Anthology of articles dealing with King's life as a rights leader, a minister, and a practioner of Gandhian non-violence.

*Preston, Edward. Martin Luther King; Fighter for Freedom. Garden City, N. Y.: Doubleday & Company, Inc., 1968.
The major aspects of King's career are discussed.

Ramachandram, G., and T. K. Mahadevan. Nonviolence After Gandhi; A Study of Martin Luther King, Jr. New Delhi: Gandhi Peace Foundation, 1968.
Analysis of King's commitment to a policy of non-violence and the effects of his death on the use of non-violence and the rights movement.

Reddick, L. D. Crusader Without Violence: A Biography of Martin Luther King, Jr. New York: Harper & Brothers, Publishers, 1959.
The earliest full-length biography of King; it contains good coverage of his youth, education, the Montgomery bus boycott, and the events that followed.

Rowe, Jeanne A. An Album of Martin Luther King, Jr. New York: Franklin Watts, Inc., 1970.
Pictorial biography of King.

Schulke, Flip, ed. Martin Luther King, Jr.: A Documentary ... Montgomery to Memphis. New York: W. W. Norton & Company, Inc., 1976.
Pictorial biography of King from the boycott to his assassination.

Slack, Kenneth. Martin Luther King. London: SCM Press, Ltd., 1970.
Analysis of King's significance to the civil rights movement and to the world.

Smith, Kenneth L., and Ira G. Zepp, Jr. Search for the Beloved Community: The Thinking of Martin Luther King, Jr. Valley Forge, Pa.: Judson Press, 1974.
Analysis of the development of King's thinking from

32 / Martin Luther King, Jr.

his study of George Davis, Walter Rauschenbusch, Reinhold Niebuhr and Gandhi.

*Stevenson, Janet. The Montgomery Bus Boycott. New York:
Franklin Watts, Inc. , 1971.
The story of the boycott and King's rise to national
recognition as a rights leader.

Walton, Hanes, Jr. The Political Philosophy of Martin
Luther King, Jr. Westport, Conn.: Greenwood Press,
1971.
Analysis of King's socio-political thinking and how
he put that philosophy to work in the rights movement.

Westin, Alan F. , and Barry Mahoney. Trial of Martin Luther
King. New York: Thomas Y. Crowell, 1974.
The story of King's arrest during the Birmingham
campaign, his conviction and the eventual Supreme Court
decision which upheld that conviction.

Williams, John A. The King God Didn't Save; Reflections on
the Life and Death of Martin Luther King, Jr. New
York: Coward-McCann, Inc. , 1970.
Unsympathetic biography of King.

*Wilson, Beth P. Martin Luther King, Jr. New York: G. P.
Putnam's Sons, 1971.
Biographical treatment of the major aspects of King's
career.

*Young, Margaret B. The Picture Life of Martin Luther King,
Jr. New York: Franklin Watts, Inc. , 1968.
Pictorial biography of King.

PERIODICAL ARTICLES

"Accident in Harlem. " Time, LXXII (September 29, 1958),
p. 14.
Report of King's stabbing in a Harlem department
store.

"The Aim: Registration. " Time, LXXXV (January 29, 1965),
   p. 20-21.
      King prepares for the voter registration drive in
   Selma.

"'Albany Movement. '" Newsweek, LVIII (December 25, 1961),
   p. 17-18.
      Report of King's arrest in Albany.

"As Negro Unrest Continues to Spread. " U. S. News & World
   Report, LXI (July 25, 1966), p. 30.
      Racial violence plagues King's housing campaign in
   Chicago.

"As 150, 000 Said Farewell to Dr. King. " U. S. News &
   World Report, LXIV (April 22, 1968), p. 38-39.
      Report of King's funeral.

"The Assassination. " Time, XCI (April 12, 1968), p. 18-19.
      Report of King's assassination and early memorials
   to him.

"Assassination Shocks the Nation. " Senior Scholastic, XCII
   (April 25, 1968), p. 18-19.
      Report of King's death and funeral.

"At the Breaking Point. " Time, LXXXVIII (July 15, 1966),
   p. 15-16.
      King warns of a possible split in the rights move-
   ment between moderate and radical forces.

"Atlanta Rose to the Occasion. " Christian Century, LXXXII
   (February 10, 1965), p. 164.
      Atlanta turns out to honor King.

"Attack on the Conscience. " Time, LXIX (February 18,
   1957), p. 17-20.
      Discussion of King's rise to leadership in the rights
   movement and his use of non-violence.

"The Awful Roar. " Time, LXXXII (August 30, 1963), p. 9-
   14.
      King's role in the Washington march.

"Back on the Home Front. " Time, LXXXII (December 27,
   1963), p. 17.
      King and the rights drive in Atlanta.

"Back with Humility. " Time, LXVIII (November 26, 1956),
    p. 20.
        King's statement on the legal victory in the bus boy-
cott.

Baldwin, James.   "The Dangerous Road Before Martin Luther
    King. " Harper's, CCXXII (February, 1961), p. 33-42.
        King seen as being able to fill the gap between Black
youth and the established leadership (NAACP).

Balk, Alfred.   "What Memorial to Martin Luther King?"
    Saturday Review, LI (May 4, 1968), p. 18.
        King's goal of racial equality and justice should not
go unfulfilled.

Barrett, Catherine O'C.   "Dr. Martin Luther King, Jr. "
    New York State Education, LV (May, 1968), p. 6.
        Memorial speech for King delivered by the president
of the New York State Teachers Association.

Belafonte, Harry.   "Martin Luther King and W. E. B. DuBois:
    A Personal Tribute. " Freedomways, XII (Winter, 1972),
    p. 17-21.
        Discussion of King's vision and hope that racial
equality could be achieved.

Bennett, John C.   "Martin Luther King, Jr. , 1929-1968. "
    Christianity and Crisis, XXVIII (April 15, 1968), p. 69-
    70.
        Memorial address for King by the editor of Chris-
tianity and Crisis.

Bennett, Lerone, Jr.   "The King Plan for Freedom. " Ebony,
    XI (July, 1956), p. 65-69. (Reprinted in Ebony, XXXI
    (November, 1975), p. 91-93.)
        King outlines an eight-point plan to end segregation.

_____.   "The Martyrdom of Martin Luther King, Jr. "
    Ebony, XXIII (May, 1968), p. 174-81+.
        The events in Memphis that brought King there, and
those that led to his assassination.

_____, and Allan Morrison.   "The South and the Negro. "
    Ebony, XII (April, 1957), p. 77+.
        Herman Talmadge defends the South, while King at-
tacks the traditional patterns of segregation.

"Beyond the Call of Duty. " Economist, CCLVII (November 29, 1975), p. 72.
Report of FBI harassment of King.

"The Big Five in Civil Rights. " Time, LXXXI (June 28, 1963), p. 16.
Discussion of King and other rights leaders.

"Biography of Martin Luther King, Jr. " Negro History Bulletin, XXXI (May, 1968), p. 3.
A short biography of King.

"Birmingham, a City. " Commonweal, LXXVIII (May 17, 1963), p. 212-13.
King's activities during the Birmingham campaign.

"Birmingham Revisited. " Time, XC (November 10, 1967), p. 28-29.
King goes to jail after an earlier conviction is upheld by the Supreme Court.

"Black Power for Whom?" Christian Century, LXXXIII (July 20, 1966), p. 903-4.
King cites practical and moral reasons for his opposition to "Black Power. "

"Black Power Play. " Economist, CCXX (July 2, 1966), p. 39.
King confronts "Black Power" advocates.

Booker, Simeon. "50, 000 March on Montgomery. " Ebony, XX (May, 1965), p. 46-48+.
King and the Selma-Montgomery march.

"Boomerang in 'Neverland, ' Selma. " Senior Scholastic, LXXXVI (March 25, 1965), p. 17-18.
King and the voter registration drive in Selma.

Bosmajian, Haig A. "Rhetoric of Martin Luther King's Letter From Birmingham Jail. " Midwest Quarterly, VIII (January, 1967), p. 127-43.
Analysis of King's letter in which he sets forth the objectives of the rights struggle.

Brennecke, Harry E. "Memorial to Dr. King. " Negro History Bulletin, XXXI (May, 1968), p. 8.
Poetic tribute to King.

Bryan, G. McLeod. "The Strength to Love Versus the Urge to Hate; A Comparison of James Baldwin and Martin Luther King from Their Writings. " Foundations, VII (April, 1964), p. 145-57.
　　King's belief in the American dream is compared with Baldwin's rejection of it.

Buckley, William F. , Jr. "On Bugging Martin Luther King. " National Review, XXI (July 15, 1969), p. 714.
　　Calls for a Congressional investigation of the wiretap of King's phone.

"Bus Boycott Leader Guilty. " Senior Scholastic, LXVIII (April 5, 1956), p. 16-17.
　　King is convicted in charges emanating from the Montgomery boycott.

Caldwell, Gilbert H. "Dreamers, Visionaries, and Prophets. " Christian Century, XCIII (March 31, 1976), p. 308-10.
　　Tribute to King's vision and his work to accomplish it.

"Can Negro Leaders Hold the Line?" Christian Century, LXXX (July 3, 1963), p. 853-84.
　　Can King and his non-violent philosophy hold back the increase of racial violence?

"Central Point. " Time, LXXXV (March 19, 1965), p. 23-28.
　　King and the voter registration drive in Selma.

Chandler, Russell. "King in the Capital. " Christianity Today, XII (January 5, 1968), p. 44-46.
　　King lays plans for the Poor People's March.

"Civil Rights Bill Moves to Fore. " Christian Century, LXXIV (June 5, 1957), p. 700.
　　King speaks before the Lincoln Memorial in support of pending civil rights legislation.

Clark, Kenneth B. "The Civil Rights Movement: Momentum and Organization. " Daedalus, XCV (Winter, 1966), p. 239-67.
　　A history of the SCLC and King's role in it.

Clarke, James W. , and John W. Soule. "How Southern Children Felt About King's Death. " Transaction, V (October, 1968), p. 35-40.

Reactions by over 300 children to King's assassination.

Clausen, Carl. "Tribute to Dr. King." Instructor, LXXXI (January, 1972), p. 78.
A second-grade class learns of King's death.

Claytor, Helen J. "Martin Luther King: The Right Man at the Right Time." YWCA Magazine (June, 1968), p. 4.
Comments about King's historical significance in tribute to King.

Cleghorn, Reese. "Martin Luther King, Jr.; Apostle of Crisis." Saturday Evening Post, CCXXXVI (June 15, 1963), p. 15-19.
Discussion of King's leadership in the Birmingham campaign.

"Confusing the Cause." Time, LXXXVI (July 16, 1965), p. 20.
King comments about his involvement with other issues.

"Connor and King." Newsweek, LXI (April 22, 1963), p. 28+.
King confronts "Bull" Connor in Birmingham.

Cook, Bruce. "King in Chicago." Commonweal, LXXXIV (April 29, 1966), p. 175-77.
King's housing drive in Chicago marks a new era in the civil rights movement.

Cook, Samuel D. "Is Martin Luther King, Jr., Irrelevant?" New South, XXVI (Spring, 1971), p. 2-14.
King's legacy will live as long as people continue to seek racial equality and justice.

_____. "Martin Luther King." Journal of Negro History, LIII (October, 1968), p. 348-54.
A tribute to King.

"Court v. King." Time, LXXXIX (June 23, 1967), p. 20.
The Supreme Court upholds King's earlier conviction in Birmingham.

"Crisis in Civil Rights." Time, LXXVII (June 2, 1961), p. 14-18.
King speaks in Montgomery in support of the Freedom Riders.

"A Critique of Martin Luther King's Social Philosophy. " Current Digest of Soviet Press, XVII (September 22, 1965), p. 7-11.
   Discussion of the development of King's philosophy and how he uses it.

"Crossing the Red Sea. " Time, LXXXVIII (September 2, 1966), p. 19.
   King leads a housing demonstration in Cicero, Ill.

"Crusade to Topple King. " Time, CVI (December 1, 1975), p. 11-12.
   Report of FBI activities involving King.

Daniel, Bradford.   "Martin Luther King Says: 'I'd Do It All Again. '" Sepia, X (December, 1961), p. 15-19.
   Portrait of King at work and at home in Atlanta.

Detwiler, Bruce.   "King/The Establishment Embrace. " Liberation, XIII (April, 1968), p. 16-17.
   King had become less effective as a rights leader prior to his death because he was seen as supporting the Establishment.

Dikshit, Om.   "Impact of Mahatma Gandhi on Martin Luther King, Jr. " Negro History Bulletin, XXXVIII (February, 1975), p. 342-44.
   Discussion of King's adaptation and use of Gandhian ideals.

"Dispute Between Hoover and King: The FBI's Answer to Criticisms. " U. S. News & World Report, LVII (December 7, 1964), p. 46+.
   The FBI tries to document some inconsistencies in King's statement.

"Dr. King. " National Review, XX (April 23, 1968), p. 376-79.
   King's assassination and the aftereffects.

"Doctor King and the Paris Press. " America, CXIII (November 13, 1965), p. 560.
   King speaks in Paris about the search for justice and the uses of non-violence.

"Dr. King Carries Fight to Northern Slums. " Ebony, XXI (April, 1966), p. 94-96+.

Report of King's plans to take his rights campaign
to the urban ghettos of the North.

"Dr. King's 'Boycott.'" Senior Scholastic, XC (April 21,
1967), p. 15-16.
An assessment of King's anti-war position.

"Dr. King's Case for Nonviolence." America, CXV (November 12, 1966), p. 578.
King reaffirms his position on non-violence.

"Dr. King's Crusade: How He Hopes to End the War." U. S.
News & World Report, LXII (May 8, 1967), p. 14.
King's efforts in the anti-war campaign.

"Dr. King's Disservice to His Cause." Life, LXII (April 21,
1967), p. 4.
Editorial comment critical of King's anti-war statement.

"Dr. King's Legacy." Commonweal, LXXXVIII (April 19,
1968), p. 125-26.
King's death seen as the time to turn back the rising
tide of violent protest without jeopardizing the search for
justice and equality.

"Dr. King's Nobel Prize." America, CXI (October 31, 1964),
p. 503.
King is named to receive the Nobel Peace Prize.

"Dr. King's Policy: Invitation to Racial Violence?" U. S.
News & World Report, LIX (October 4, 1965), p. 22.
King held responsible for crimes stemming from the
rights struggle.

"Dr. Martin Luther King, Jr." Weekly Compilation of Presidential Documents, IV (April 8, 1968), p. 640-1.
Text of President Johnson's statement on the death
of King and his proclamation for a national day of mourning.

"Dogs, Kids, and Clubs." Time, LXXXI (May 10, 1963), p.
19.
Police break-up King's demonstration in Birmingham.

Douglas, Carlyle C. "Ralph Abernathy; The Man Who Fights
to Keep King's Dream Alive." Ebony, XXV (January,

1970), p. 40-46+.
King's relationship with Abernathy is discussed.

Driscoll, Edward A. "Antitrespass Law Invoked. " Christian
Century, LXXVII (November 30, 1960), p. 1417.
Report of King's arrest in Atlanta.

Duggan, William R. "Three Men of Peace. " Crisis, LXXXI
(December, 1974), p. 331-34.
Analysis of the non-violence of King. Gandhi, and
Albert Luthuli of South Africa.

Dunbar, Ernest. "A Visit with Martin Luther King. " Look,
XXVII (February 12, 1963), p. 92-96.
King comments on the status of the rights movement
and his role in the struggle.

"Eight Days in Ga. Jails Leave Rev. King Unbowed. " Jet,
XIX (November 10, 1960), p. 4-5.
King is released after his arrest for trespassing.

Elder, John D. "Martin Luther King and American Civil
Religion. " Harvard Divinity School Bulletin, I (Spring,
1968), p. 17-18.
King's use of Biblical symbols and his non-violent
philosophy are seen as contributions to civil religion.

"End of the Road?" Time, XC (August 25, 1967), p. 18.
King tries to hold back extremism in his campaign
in urban ghettos.

"Endorse Dr. King for Nobel Prize. " Christian Century,
LXXXI (August 12, 1964), p. 1006.
Christian Century supports King for the Nobel Peace
Prize.

"Equality Is Not Negotiable. " Christian Century, LXXX (Sep-
tember 4, 1963), p. 1069-70.
Report of appearance by King and Roy Wilkins on
"Meet the Press" prior to the Washington march.

"'Even If I Die in the Struggle. '" U. S. News & World Report,
LXIV (April 15, 1968), p. 33.
Biographical sketch of King.

"The Execution of Dr. King. " Ramparts, VI (May, 1968), p.
46-47.

Editorial comment about King's death and the ideas
he had used in the rights struggle.

"The FBI and Civil Rights. " U. S. News & World Report,
LVII (November 30, 1964), p. 56-58.
J. Edgar Hoover comments about the rights move-
ment and King, and King responds to Hoover's statement.

Fager, Charles E. "Dilemma for Dr. King. " Christian Cen-
tury, LXXXIII (March 16, 1966), p. 331-32.
The war poses a moral or economic problem for
King.

Fairlie, Henry. "Martin Luther King. " Encounter, XXX
(June, 1968), p. 3-6.
King's importance seen as his being able to retain
leadership of the rights movement for 13 years.

"Farewell to a 'Drum Major for Justice and Peace. '" Freedomways, VIII (Spring, 1968), p. 101-2.
Editorial comment about the loss of King and his
impact on the rights movement.

Fey, Harold E. "Negro Ministers Arrested. " Christian Century, LXXIII (March 7, 1956), p. 294-95.
Report of King's arrest in Montgomery.

"Four Poets on Martin Luther King. " Nation, CCVI (June
24, 1968), p. 831.
Four poets pay tribute to King.

Frazier, Arthur, and Virgil Roberts. "A Discourse on Black
Nationalism. " American Behavioral Scientist, XII (March-
April, 1969), p. 50-56.
King seen as dominant figure during the non-violent
era of the rights movement.

"A Freedom Budget for the Poor. " Business Week, May 4,
1968, p. 68+.
King's economic ideas of income maintenance and
guaranteed employment.

"Freedom--Now. " Time, LXXXI (May 17, 1963), p. 23-25.
King and the Birmingham campaign.

Freeman, Harry. "Freedom Now; Negro Liberation Movement Enters a New Phase. " New Times, September 11,

1963, p. 12-13.
Report on King and the Washington march.

"'Full-scale Assault.'" Newsweek, LV (February 29, 1960),
p. 24-25.
King discusses the use of the sit-in and plans to seek
integration at all levels of society.

"Future of Black Leadership." Time, XCIII (April 4, 1969),
p. 29-30.
Time essay on finding a leader to assume King's
role.

Galphin, Bruce M. "Political Future of Dr. King." Nation,
CXCIII (September 23, 1961), p. 177-80.
King could alter the political course of the South and
the country if he could organize the Black voting bloc.
This article was reprinted as "Does Martin Luther King
Have a Future in Politics?" Negro Digest, XI (January,
1962), p. 41-47.

"A Gandhi Society?" Christian Century, LXXIX (June 13,
1962), p. 735-36.
King's relationship with the Gandhi Society for Human
Rights.

"Gandhi Society Explained." Christian Century, LXXIX (August
1, 1962), p. 929-30.
King explains he can be affiliated with the Gandhi Society without a loss of Christian faith.

Garland, Phyllis. "'I've Been to the Mountaintop.'" Ebony,
XXIII (May, 1968), p. 124-36+.
Discussion of his career and accomplishments as a
tribute to King.

"Georgia Imprisons Martin Luther King, Jr." Christian Century, LXXVII (November 9, 1960), p. 1300.
King arrested in Atlanta for driving without a Georgia
license.

"Georgia Justice." Nation, CXCI (November 5, 1960), p.
338-39.
King arrested for driving without a Georgia license
and then for trespassing.

"Georgia Whodunit." Newsweek, LX (July 23, 1962), p. 18-
19.

Anonymous benefactor pays King's bail out of an Albany jail.

Good, Paul. "Chicago Summer: Bossism, Racism and Dr. King. " Nation, CCIII (September 19, 1966), p. 237-42.
King wins some concessions from Mayor Daley.

"A Good Journey to Martin Luther King, Jr. " Liberation, III (February, 1959), p. 19.
Editorial in support of King's journey to India.

Goodman, George. "Dr. King, One Year After 'He Lives, Man!'" Look, XXXIII (April 15, 1969), p. 29-31.
King's ideas are still alive.

"The Government and Martin Luther King. " Atlantic, CCXXVI (November, 1970), p. 43-52.
Discussion of the FBI's bugging of King's phone.

"Graham and King as Ghetto-mates. " Christian Century, LXXXIII (August 10, 1966), p. 976.
A suggestion that King and Billy Graham work together for racial and social justice.

"A Great Ride. " Time, LXVIII (December 31, 1956), p. 10.
King and Rosa Parks board a Montgomery bus as the boycott ends.

Griffin, John H. "Martin Luther King's Moment. " Sign, XLII (April, 1963), p. 28-31+.
King's early efforts in the Civil Rights movement.

Halberstam, David. "Notes from the Bottom of the Mountain. " Harper's Bazaar, CCXXXVI (June, 1968), p. 40-42.
A memorial to King.

_____ . "The Second Coming of Martin Luther King. " Harper's Bazaar, CCXXXV (August, 1967), p. 39-51.
King takes his rights campaign to the urban ghettos of the North.

Hammer, Richard. "The Life and Death of Martin Luther King. " Midstream, XIV (May, 1968), p. 3-16.
Biography of King and a discussion of his philosophy.

Harper, Fredrick D. "Influence of Martin Luther King on Education. " Adult Education, XXI (April, 1973), p. 310-12+.

Analysis of King's influence on education, which he saw as a key to a better life.

"Heat on Highway 51." Time, LXXXVII (June 17, 1966), p. 26-27.
King marches in Mississippi after James Meredith is ambushed.

Herberg, Will. "A Religious 'Right' to Violate the Law?" National Review, XVI (July 14, 1964), p. 579-80.
Opposition to King's view that civil disobedience has roots in Christian theology and ethics.

Herbers, John. "Critical Test for the Nonviolent Way." New York Times Magazine, July 5, 1964, p. 5+.
King's philosophy put to the test in St. Augustine.

"A Hero to Be Remembered." Ebony, XXX (April, 1975), p. 134-35.
Editorial comment on the seventh anniversary of King's death.

"The Hoover-King Meeting." Newsweek, LXIV (December 14, 1964), p. 22+.
King and J. Edgar Hoover meet to end the disagreement between the FBI and the civil rights movement.

"An Hour of Need." Time, XCI (April 12, 1968), p. 17.
Discussion of King's assassination.

"How Martin Luther King Won the Nobel Peace Prize." U.S. News & World Report, LVIII (February 8, 1965), p. 76-77.
The Nobel committee explains its selection of King.

Howard, Ruth. "Requiem to Dr. Martin Luther King, Jr." Negro History Bulletin, XXXII (April, 1969), p. 17.
Poetic tribute to King.

Hughes, Emmet J. "A Curse of Confusion." Newsweek, LXIX (May 1, 1967), p. 17.
Editorial comment against King's anti-war position.

"Incident in Harlem." Newsweek, LII (September 29, 1958), p. 24.
Report of King's stabbing in Harlem department store.

"International Evening: Martin Luther King." Publishers'
Weekly, CXCI (June 19, 1967), p. 52.
King speaks at a reception given by Harper & Row
publishing house.

"Is It Right to Break the Law?" U. S. News & World Report,
LV (August 12, 1963), p. 6.
King affirms his theory of civil disobedience, while
a judge offers an opposing view.

"Is Vietnam to Become a 'Civil Rights' Issue?" U. S. News
& World Report, LIX (July 19, 1965), p. 12.
King urges that negotiations be opened with North
Vietnam.

"'It Ain't No Vaudeville.'" New Republic, CXXXIV (April 2,
1956), p. 5.
Report of King's arrest in Montgomery.

"I've Been to the Mountaintop." Life, LXIV (April 12, 1968),
p. 74-80+.
Discussion of King's life, his accomplishments, and
his assassination.

"'I've Been to the Mountaintop.'" Newsweek, LXXI (April 15,
1968), p. 38.
A chronological listing of King's major accomplishments.

Izakov, Boris. "Who Killed Dr. King?" New Times, May
29, 1968, p. 14-16.
An assessment of the facts in King's assassination.

Jack, Homer H. "Conversation in Ghana." Christian Century, LXXIV (April 10, 1957), p. 446-48.
King attends the independence celebration in Ghana.

Jet, XXXIV (April 18, 1968 and April 25, 1968).
Both issues are entirely devoted to articles about
King's life, his family, the assassination and funeral,
and the effects of his death. Though many of these articles are individually cited, they are not all included.

"Just How Many Stokelys?" Economist, CCXXVII (April 13,
1968), p. 16-17.
King's death is seen against a backdrop of increasing
violence in racial matters.

"Johnson, King, and Ho Chi Minh. " Christianity Today, XII
(April 26, 1968), p. 24-25.
Editorial comment about King's death and violence in
America.

Kempton, Murray. "Among School Children. " Spectator,
CCX (May 10, 1963), p. 593-94.
King and the Birmingham campaign.

King, Coretta S. "He Had a Dream. " Life, LXVII (September 12, 1969), p. 54-54B+.
An excerpt from My Life with Martin Luther King.

_____. "'How Many Men Must Die?'" Life, LXIV (April
19, 1968), p. 34-35.
An excerpt from Mrs. King's address before a crowd
in Memphis after Martin's death.

_____. "The Legacy of Martin Luther King, Jr.: The
Church in Action. " Theology Today, XXVII (July, 1970),
p. 129-39.
Discussion of King's legacy in the struggle for freedom and equality.

_____. "My Dream for My Children. " Good Housekeep-
ing, CLVIII (June, 1964), p. 77+.
King's career and its effect upon his family.

"King. " New Yorker, XLI (May 1, 1965), p. 35-37.
King address to the Bar Association of New York.

"King Acts for Peace. " Christian Century, LXXXII (September 29, 1965), p. 1180-81.
Reaction to King's anti-war position.

"King Announces Plan to Move to Atlanta. " Southern School
News, VI (January, 1960), p. 9.
King moves to Atlanta to direct national campaign for
integration.

"King Comes to Chicago. " Christian Century, LXXXII (August 11, 1965), p. 979-80.
King goes to Chicago to aid in protest for the re-
moval of the Superintendent of Education.

"'King Is the Man, Oh Lord. '" Newsweek, LXXI (April 15,
1968), p. 34-38.

Discussion of the events leading up to King's death.

"King Led Civil Rights Fight from Montgomery to Memphis. "
Jet, XXXIV (April 18, 1968), p. 14-21.
  An account of King's life as a rights leader.

"King Moves North. " Time, LXXXV (April 30, 1965), p. 32-
33.
  King takes his rights campaign to New York and Boston.

"King Off Centre. " Economist, CCVII (April 20, 1963), p.
234.
  King's timing in the Birmingham campaign is ques-
tioned.

"King on the Fence. " Economist, CCXXI (October 22, 1966),
p. 370-73.
  King's name doesn't appear with other Black leaders
in ad repudiating the use of violence in rights activities.

"King Proposed for Peace Prize. " Christian Century, LXXIX
(February 12, 1964), p. 198.
  King is nominated for the Nobel Peace Prize.

"King Receives Nobel Prize. " Christian Century, LXXXI
(October 28, 1964), p. 1324.
  King receives the Nobel Peace Prize and promises
to give the money to the SCLC.

"King Speaks for Peace. " Christian Century, LXXXIV (April
19, 1967), p. 492-93.
  King speaks out against the war in Vietnam.

"King Takes to the Slums. " Economist, CCXVIII (February
5, 1966), p. 509.
  King works to improve ghetto conditions in Chicago.

"King Wants White Demonstrators. " Christian Century, LXXXI
(June 3, 1964), p. 724-25.
  King says he wants white rights workers.

"King's Death Stuns Nation; Troops Quell Disturbances. "
Congressional Quarterly Weekly Report, XXVI (April 12,
1968), p. 817-20.
  King's assassination and the aftereffects.

48 / Martin Luther King, Jr.

"King's Dream Recaptured. " Christianity Today, XIV (April
10, 1970), p. 45.
Discussion of the film "King: A Filmed Record ...
Montgomery to Memphis, " a filmed biography of King.

"King's Last March. " Time, XCI (April 19, 1968), p. 18-19.
Report of King's funeral.

"King's Last March: 'We Lost Somebody. '" Newsweek, LXXI
(April 22, 1968), p. 26-31.
Report of King's funeral.

"King's Last Tape. " Newsweek, LXXII (December 16, 1968),
p. 34+.
Excerpts from King's last article, which appeared in
the January, 1969, Playboy.

"King's Targets. " Newsweek, LXIII (June 22, 1964), p. 26+.
King takes his rights drive to Tuscaloosa, Ala. , and
St. Augustine.

Kopkind, Andrew. "The American Nightmare. " New Statesman, LXXV (April 12, 1968), p. 471-72.
Reflections on the significance of King's assassination.

Lantz, Ragni. "Threats from 'Some of Our Sick White
Brother' Didn't Stop Him. " Jet, XXXIV (April 18, 1968),
p. 4-11.
King's presence in Memphis and the eventual assassination.

"Learning to Live With Riots. " Economist, CCXXVII (April
13, 1968), p. 23-24.
King's assassination and the aftereffects.

"The Legacy of Martin Luther King. " Business Week, April
13, 1968, p. 144.
Editorial tribute to King, praising his philosophy and
the things he accomplished with it.

"The Legacy of Martin Luther King. " Life, LXIV (April 19,
1968), p. 4.
Editorial tribute to King, his vision and his dream
are his legacy.

Leonard, Edward A. "Nonviolence and Violence in American

Racial Protests, 1942-1967." Rocky Mountain Social Science Journal, VI (1969), p. 10-22.
Discussion of King's role as the leader of the non-violent forces of the rights movement.

Leonard, George B. "Who Will Count His Vote?" Look, XXXII (August 20, 1968), p. 22-23.
A tribute to King and the role he could have played in the upcoming elections.

Levine, Richard. "Jesse Jackson: Heir to Dr. King?" Harper, CCXXXVIII (March, 1969), 58-70.
Discussion of King's relationship with Jesse Jackson.

"Life and Death of Martin Luther King." Christianity Today, XII (April 26, 1968), p. 37-40.
A brief description of the highlights of King's career.

Lomax, Louis E. "The Negro Revolt Against 'The Negro Leaders.'" Harper, CCXX (June, 1960), p. 41-48.
King seen as part of a leadership that's challenging the position of established leaders like the NAACP.

Long, Margaret. "Martin Luther King, Jr.: He Kept So Plain." Progressive, XXXII (May, 1968), p. 20-24.
Memorial article to King, who the author saw as withstanding the pressures of the fame he had gained and being able to maintain his true self.

_____. "The Unity of the Rifting Negro Movement." Progressive, XXVIII (February, 1964), p. 10-14.
Discussion of the relationship between the major groups and their leaders within the rights movement.

"'Long Live the King.'" Newsweek, XLVII (April 2, 1956), p. 26.
King jailed for his activities in the Montgomery boycott.

"The Long March." Time, LXXXI (June 21, 1963), p. 13-17.
King discusses the status of the rights struggle, its future plans, and other topics.

"Lord of the Doves." Newsweek, LXIX (April 17, 1967), p. 44+.
King delivers his anti-war address at the Riverside Church.

Maguire, John D. "Martin Luther King and Viet Nam. "
Christianity and Crisis, XXVII (May 1, 1967), p. 89-90.
A reply to the criticism of King's anti-war state-
ments.

_____. "Martin Luther King, Jr. , 1929-1968. " Chris-
tianity and Crisis, XXVIII (April 15, 1968), p. 69.
Memorial article to King.

"Man of Conflict Wins a Peace Prize. " U. S. News & World
Report, LVII (October 26, 1964), p. 24.
Report of King's being awarded the Nobel Peace Prize.

"Man of the Year. " Nation, CXCVIII (January 13, 1964), p.
41-42.
Editorial support of King's selection as Time's Man
of the Year.

"Man of the Year. " Time, LXXXIII (January 3, 1964), p.
13-27.
King selected by Time as Man of the Year; biographical material is included in the report.

"March on Washington--What to Expect. " U. S. News &
World Report, LXIV (March 18, 1968), p. 44.
King discusses plans for the proposed Poor People's
march.

"The March to Montgomery. " Senior Scholastic, LXXXVI
(April 1, 1965), p. 8+.
King on the Selma-Montgomery march.

"The March's Meaning. " Time, LXXXII (September 6, 1963),
p. 13-15.
Report on the Washington march and King's speech.

"Martin Luther King. " Nation, CCVI (April 15, 1968), p.
490.
Editorial in memorial to King.

"Martin Luther King. " Reporter, XXXVIII (April 18, 1968),
p. 10.
King's work must be continued as a memorial to him.

"Martin Luther King, Jr. , and Mahatma Gandhi. " Negro
History Bulletin, XXXI (May, 1968), p. 4-5.
Editorial on King's use of Gandhian methods in the

struggle for equality and justice.

"Martin Luther King, Jr.: Man of 1963. " Negro History
    Bulletin, XXVII (June, 1964), p. 136-37.
        King honored upon his selection by Time as Man of
    the Year.

"Martin Luther King, Jr.: 1929-1968. " Merchandising Week,
    C (April 8, 1968), p. 3.
        Editorial tribute to King and a call for support of the
    sanitation strike in Memphis and passage of civil rights
    legislation as memorials to King.

"Martin Luther King, We Shall Overcome. " UNESCO Couri-
    er, XXII (October, 1969), p. 20-21.
        A tribute to King and his philosophy of non-violence.

"Martin Luther King: Who He Is ... What He Believes. "
    U. S. News & World Report, LVIII (April 5, 1965), p. 18.
        Biographical sketch of King.

"Martin Luther King's Tropic Interlude. " Ebony, XXII (June,
    1967), p. 112-14+.
        King vacations in Jamaica while finishing Where Do
    We Go from Here: Chaos or Community?

"Martyrdom Comes to America's Moral Leader. " Christian
    Century, LXXXV (April 17, 1968), p. 475.
        Reflections upon King's life and accomplishments,
    and what to expect after his death.

"Martyrdom of Martin Luther King, Jr. " Crisis, LXXV
    (April, 1968), p. 114-15.
        Editorial tribute to King.

Massey, James E.   "The Relational Imperative. " Spectrum,
    XLVII (July, 1971), p. 14-17.
        Discussion of King's theological understanding.

Maureen, Sister Mary.   "A Man Named Martin. " Marist,
    XX (May-June, 1964), p. 44-47.
        [Not examined.]

Mays, Dr. Benjamin E.   "Eulogy. " Negro History Bulletin,
    XXXI (May, 1968), p. 24.
        Mays' eulogy delivered at King's funeral.

Meagher, Sylvia. "Two Assassinations." Minority of One, X (June, 1968), p. 9-10.
A comparison of the deaths of King and John Kennedy.

Meier, August. "On the Role of Martin Luther King." New Politics, IV (Winter, 1965), p. 52-59.
Discussion of King's philosophy, his activities in the rights struggle, and the reasons for his success.

"Memo to Martin Luther King." National Review, XIX (December 12, 1967), p. 1368-69.
King plans further rights activities in Northern cities.

"Memphis March Leads to Riot." Senior Scholastic, XCII (April 11, 1968), p. 22-23.
Report of King's march in Memphis that ended as a violent riot.

Meyer, Frank S. "Principles and Heresies." National Review, XX (January 16, 1968), p. 36.
King seen as a militant behind a cloak of non-violence.

_____. "The Violence of Nonviolence." National Review, XVII (April 20, 1965), p. 327.
Criticism of King and his non-violent methods.

Miller, James A. "Martin Luther King, Jr.; The End of an Era." Black Academy Review, I (Fall, 1970), p. 27-34.
A review of King's career from the vision he started with to the direction he was headed before his death.

Montagu, Ashley. "The Saturday Review-Anisfield-Wolf Awards." Saturday Review, XLII (May 30, 1959), p. 12-13.
King receives an award for Stride Toward Freedom.

Morgan, Thomas B. "What's Next for the Civil-Rights Movement: Requiem or Revival?" Look, XXX (June 14, 1966), p. 70-73+.
King begins his housing drive in Chicago.

Morris, Steve. "Violence Stalked Nonviolent Leader During His Career." Jet, XXXIV (April 18, 1968), p. 46-48.
A chronology of attempts on King's life and outbreaks of violence during his campaigns.

Mukerji, Rose. "When Words Fail ... Dance." Childhood

Education, XLVI (April, 1970), p. 374-75.
    Reactions to King's death by six-year olds.

"A Negro and Negroes. " Newsweek, LI (February 24, 1958),
    p. 32.
    King speaks in Greensboro, N. C. , on gaining the
respect of Whites.

"Negroes Press for Showdown in South. " Business Week,
    May 11, 1963, p. 24-26.
    King urges an economic boycott in Alabama.

Nelson, Harold A.   "The Re-education of Sociologists: A
    Note on the Impact of Dr. Martin Luther King, Jr. , as
    Educator. " Journal of Human Relations, XVI (1968), p.
    514-23.
    King changes attitudes held by sociologists about
ethnic relations.

Nelson, William S.   "Martin Luther King. "   Political Science
    Review, IX (January-June, 1970), p. 166-72.
    Tribute to King and his non-violent philosophy.

"New Negro Threat: Mass Disobedience. " U. S. News &
    World Report, LXIII (August 28, 1967), p. 10.
    King plans to increase rights drive in the North.

"The New Racism. " Time, LXXXVIII (July 1, 1966), p. 11-
    13.
    King confronts "Black Power" in Mississippi.

"New Sounds in a Courthouse. " Time, LXVII (April 2, 1956),
    p. 24.
    King's trial in Montgomery.

"New Tack for Dr. King. " U. S. News & World Report,
    LVIII (May 3, 1965), p. 18.
    King becomes involved with the anti-war movement.

"No False Moves for King. " Christian Century, LXXX (July
    17, 1963), p. 919.
    King is watched constantly by the press.

"No Peace for Winner of Peace Prize. " U. S. News & World
    Report, LVIII (February 1, 1965), p. 19.
    King begins the voter registration drive in Selma.

"Nobel Awards for Peace and Medicine. " Illustrated London News, CCXLV (October 24, 1964), p. 661.
Pictorial coverage of King's acceptance of the Nobel Peace Prize.

"Nobel Peace Prize Goes to Martin Luther King. " Negro History Bulletin, XXVIII (November, 1964), p. 35.
Editorial honoring King's selection for the Nobel Peace Prize.

"Nobel Prize Awards in Stockholm and Oslo. " Illustrated London News, CCXLV (December 19, 1964), p. 967.
King receives the Nobel Peace Prize.

"Nobelman King. " Newsweek, LXIV (October 26, 1964), p. 77.
King named to receive Nobel Peace Prize.

"Non-nonviolence. " Economist, CCXXVII (April 6, 1968), p. 35-36.
March led by King ends in a riot.

"Nonviolence on Trial. " Economist, CCIV (July 28, 1962), p. 354.
King puts his non-violence to the test in Albany.

"Notes and Comments. " New Yorker, XLIV (April 13, 1968), p. 35-37.
Discussion of King's philosophy and how he used it, as a tribute to him.

"Now a March of Tribute, Not Protest. " U. S. News & World Report, LIX (August 16, 1965), p. 12.
King leads a march in support of home rule proposal for the District of Columbia.

"Now, Dr. King's Marchers Turn North. " U. S. & World Report, LVIII (May 3, 1965), p. 8.
King aids school desegregation drive in Boston.

Nuby, Charolette. "He Had a Dream. " Negro History Bulletin, XXXI (May, 1968), p. 21.
Poetic tribute to King.

Oglesby, Enoch H. "Ethical and Educational Implications of Black Theology in America. " Religious Education, LXIX (July, 1974), p. 403-12.

A comparison of the theological views of King and James H. Cone.

"On to Montgomery. " Newsweek, LXV (March 29, 1965), p. 19-20.
King announces that the march to Montgomery will take place despite opposition.

"One Last Chance. " Christian Century, LXXXIII (June 22, 1966), p. 792-93.
A review of King's objectives in the Chicago rights campaign.

Padley, Robert B. , and F. M. Archer. "Nobel Prize for King?" Christian Century, LXXXI (October 21, 1964), p. 1300-2.
A suggestion that King and John Kennedy share the Nobel Peace Prize.

Parks, Gordon. "'A Man Who Tried to Love Somebody. '" Life, LXIV (April 19, 1968), p. 28-39.
Reflections on King's funeral and the aftereffects of his death.

"Peace with Justice. " Commonweal, LXXVIII (May 31, 1963), p. 268.
Comments on King's letter from a Birmingham jail.

"The Peaceful Kingdom. " National Review, XVI (December 29, 1964), p. 1135-36.
Criticism of King's statements after receiving the Nobel Peace Prize.

Peerman, Dean, and Martin E. Marty. "Selma: Sustaining the Momentum. " Christian Century, LXXXII (March 24, 1965), p. 358-60.
King appeals to the nation for aid in the Selma campaign.

Peters, William. "The Man Who Fights Hate with Love. " Redbook, CXVII (September, 1961), p. 36-37+.
Biographical portrait of King.

"Pharaoh's Lesson. " Time, LXXXVIII (September 9, 1966), p. 22.
Militant factions of the rights movement continue to pressure King.

Pilpel, Harriet F. "Copyright Case Involves 'New' Use of Material; Unauthorized Recording of Speech by Martin Luther King." Publishers Weekly, CLXXXV (April 6, 1964), p. 26.
  Report of King's copyright case involving his "I Have a Dream" speech.

"Poorly Timed Protest." Time, LXXXI (April 19, 1963), p. 30-31.
  King brings the rights drive to Birmingham.

"Pressure Is on the Diehards." Business Week, April 3, 1965, p. 27-28.
  King turns his successful rights campaign to the North.

"The Prince of Peace Is Dead." Ebony, XXIII (May, 1968), p. 172.
  Photo-editorial eulogizing King.

"The Prophetic Ministry?" Newsweek, LX (August 20, 1962), p. 78-79.
  King justifies his position as a minister with his work in the rights struggle.

"Protest on Route 80." Time, LXXXV (April 2, 1965), p. 21-22.
  King leads the Selma-Montgomery march.

Quarles, Benjamin. "Martin Luther King in History." Negro History Bulletin, XXXI (May, 1968), p. 9.
  Analysis of King's place in history.

"Race Violence Will Defeat Itself." Christian Century, LXXV (September 17, 1958), p. 1046.
  King is arrested in Montgomery.

"Rare Tribute; King Honored in Atlanta." Time, LXXXV (February 5, 1965), p. 24.
  King honored in Atlanta after receiving the Nobel Peace Prize.

Rathburn, John W. "Martin Luther King: The Theology of Social Action." American Quarterly, XX (1968), p. 38-53.
  Discussion of King's theological philosophy and how he used it in the rights struggle.

"Reactions to the Slaying of Martin Luther King. " America, CXVIII (April 20, 1968), p. 534-36.
Reactions to King's death in Chicago, Detroit, Washington, and parts of Europe.

"Rebuke to Dr. King? Negro Official Speaks Out. " U. S. News & World Report, LIX (August 30, 1965), p. 16.
Assistant Secretary of Labor George Weaver opposes King's anti-war views.

"A Remarkable Dinner and ... Off to Jail. " Life, LVIII (February 12, 1965), p. 34-34A.
King honored in Atlanta, then goes to Selma where he is arrested.

"Render Unto King. " Time, LXXXVII (March 25, 1966), p. 18-19.
King begins his open housing drive in Chicago.

Richardson, Herbert W. "Martin Luther King--Unsung Theologian. " Commonweal, LXXXVIII (May 3, 1968), p. 201-3.
Discussion of King's theological philosophy and how he used it in the rights struggle.

Roberts, Adam. "Martin Luther King and Non-violent Resistance. " World Today, XXIV (June, 1968), p. 226-36.
Discussion of King's use of non-violence in the civil rights movement.

Robins, Natalie S. "Martin Luther King. " Nation, CCX (June 22, 1970), p. 765.
Poetic tribute to King.

"Rolling On. " Time, LXXVII (June 9, 1961), p. 15-16.
Court order restrains King from encouraging Freedom Riders.

Romero, Patricia W. "Martin Luther King and His Challenge to White America. " Negro History Bulletin, XXXI (May, 1968), p. 6-8.
King's challenge is to educate Whites to the needs of the Black community.

Rose, Stephen C. "Test for Nonviolence. " Christian Century, LXXX (May 29, 1963), p. 714-16.
King is optimistic about the struggle for equality in Birmingham.

58 / Martin Luther King, Jr.

Roth, Ruth M. "Martyrdom." English Journal, LVII (November, 1968), p. 1147-48.
    An analogy is drawn between the martyrdom of King and Thomas Becket.

Rowan, Carl T. "Martin Luther King's Tragic Decision." Reader's Digest, XCI (September, 1967), p. 37-42.
    Criticism of King's anti-war position.

Rustin, Bayard. "Montgomery Diary." Liberation, I (April 1956).
    Report of King's activities during the bus boycott.

Salmans, Sandra, and Anthony Marro. "Tales of the FBI." Newsweek, LXXXVI (December 1, 1975), p. 35-36.
    Report of the FBI's investigation of King and the civil rights movement.

Sanders, Charles L. "The Tortuous Road to Oslo." Ebony, XX (March, 1965), p. 36+.
    King at the Nobel presentations and his tour of Europe.

Schrag, Peter. "The Uses of Martyrdom." Saturday Review, LI (April 20, 1968), p. 28-29.
    Tribute to King.

Schulte-Nordholt, J. W. "The Negro in the Sixties: A White and a Black Problem, or: The Circle of Prejudice." Jahrbuch Fur Amerikastudien, XV (1970), p. 38-56.
    Discussion of King's role as leader of the civil rights movement.

Schulz, William. "Martin Luther King's March on Washington." Reader's Digest, SCII (April, 1968), p. 65-69.
    Report on King's proposed Poor People's march.

Scott, Robert L. "Black Power Bends Martin Luther King." Speaker and Gavel, V (March, 1968), p. 80-86.
    Analysis of the effects of the "Black Power" movement upon King's rhetoric.

"Search for a New Selma." Newsweek, LXVI (December 20, 1965), p. 29-30.
    King plans to continue the rights drive in the South.

"Selma: Beatings Start the Savage Season." Life, LVIII

(March 19, 1965), p. 30-37.
Report on King's voter registration drive and the
first attempt to march to Montgomery.

"The Selma Campaign. " National Review, XVII (March 23,
1965), p. 227-28.
Report on the rights drive in Selma and King's use
of non-violence.

"Selma, Continued. " Time, LXXXV (February 5, 1965), p. 24.
King continues his activities in Selma.

"Shades of Black Power. " Economist, CCXX (September 3,
1966), p. 909-10.
King still a popular leader, but his methods are less
effective in the North.

"Shades of Bull Connor. " Newsweek, LXV (February 1, 1965),
p. 21-22.
Racial violence erupts as King begins the Selma campaign.

Shaffer, Helen B.   "Negro Power Struggle. " Editorial Research Reports, February 21, 1968, p. 123-40.
King involved in a power struggle with "Black Power"
advocates.

_____. "Negro Revolution: Next Steps. " Editorial Re-
search Reports, July 21, 1965, p. 525-42.
King and other leaders discuss future rights campaigns and the strategies to be used.

Sharma, Mohan L.   "Martin Luther King: Modern America's
Greatest Theologian of Social Action. " Journal of Negro
History, LIII (1968), p. 257-63.
King seen as a social theologian.

"Should the President 'Risk His Life' for Integration?" U. S.
News & World Report, LIV (June 10, 1963), p. 35-40.
King discusses the pace of school desegregation.

Sibley, Mulford Q.   "Negro Revolution and Non-Violent Action: Martin Luther King. " Political Science Review,
IX (January-June, 1970), p. 173-93.
Discussion of King's use of non-violent methods in
the civil rights struggle.

"Signs of Erosion. " Newsweek, LXIX (April 10, 1967), p. 32.
Comment about King's anti-war position.

Simon, Paul. "Montgomery Looks Forward. " Christian Century, LXXV (January 22, 1958), p. 104.
King holds the second Institute on Non-Violence and Social Change in Montgomery.

"Sit-ins and Shut Downs. " Economist, CXCVII (October 29, 1960), p. 448.
King arrested during lunch-counter demonstration in Atlanta.

Sitton, Claude. "Dr. King, Symbol of the Segregation Struggle. " New York Times Magazine, January 22, 1961, p. 10+.
Biographical portrait of King.

Smith, Donald H. "An Exegesis of Martin Luther King's Social Philosophy. " Phylon, XXXI (Spring, 1970), p. 89-97.
Analysis of King's social philosophy and how he developed it.

_____. "Martin Luther King, Jr. : In the Beginning at Montgomery. " Southern Speech Journal, XXXIV (Fall, 1968), p. 8-17.
Discussion of King's start as a leader in the rights movement.

Smith, Kenneth L. "Martin Luther King, Jr. : Reflections of a Former Teacher. " Voice of Crozer Theological Seminary, LVII (April, 1965), p. 2-3.
King's ethics teacher from his undergraduate days at Crozer Theological Seminary recalls his relationship with King, as his former student is awarded the Nobel Peace Prize.

_____, and Ira G. Zepp, Jr. "Martin Luther King's Vision of the Beloved Community. " Christian Century, XCI (April 3, 1974), p. 361-63.
Analysis of King's philosophy and the role of the "Beloved Community" within it.

Smylie, James H. "On Jesus, Pharaoh and the Chosen People. " Interpretation, XXIV (January, 1970), p. 74-91.
King seen as a Biblical interpreter and a humanist.

"Spiritual Man of the Year. " Christian Century, LXXIV (March 13, 1957), p. 331.
King is supported for ideas expressed in previous Christian Century article.

Steinkraus, Warren E. "Martin Luther King's Personalism and Nonviolence. " Journal of the History of Ideas, XXXIV (January, 1973), p. 97-111.
Discussion of the origins of King's philosophy.

Stevenson, Janet. "Rosa Parks Wouldn't Budge. " American Heritage, XXIII (February, 1972), p. 56-64+.
King's involvement in the Montgomery boycott and the start of his rights movement leadership.

"Still King. " Christian Century, LXXXIII (September 7, 1966), p. 1071.
King reaches an agreement with city leaders on the housing situation in Chicago.

"Summer Strategy. " Newsweek, LXV (April 12, 1965), p. 28-29.
King plans for demonstrations to follow the Selma-Montgomery march.

Svenio, Per. "Martin Luther King: A Creative Extremist. " Norwegian Contributions to American Studies, IV (1973), p. 361-77.
Analysis of King as a philosopher and how he employs his ideas.

"Swift Deliverance. " Time, LXXVI (November 7, 1960), p. 30.
King arrested for picketing in Decatur, Ga.

Takulia, H. S. "The Place of Martin Luther King in the Negroes' Struggle for Equality. " Political Science Review, IX (January-June, 1970), p. 136-65.
An assessment of King's role in the rights movement and his use of non-violent methods.

"The Talk Is Race. " Time, LXXXIV (August 7, 1964), p. 17-18.
King confers in New York with Mayor Robert Wagner.

Tancil, Sallie, ed. "A Children's Tribute to Dr. King. " Negro History Bulletin, XXXI (May, 1968), p. 2.

School children present a poetic tribute to King.

"Third Order Honors Dr. King." Interracial Review, XXXVI (December, 1963), p. 249.
King receives the 1963 St. Francis Peace Medal presented by the North American Federation of the Third Order of St. Francis.

Thomas, C. W. "Historical Notes; Dr. King Leads Protest March in Boston." Negro History Bulletin, XXVIII (April, 1965), p. 169.
King leads Boston demonstration and speaks about the struggle for equality and justice.

_____. "Nobel Prize Goes to Martin Luther King." Negro History Bulletin, XXVIII (November, 1964), p. 35.
Report on King being selected to receive the Nobel Peace Prize.

"Too Many Cooks, Too Much Spice." Christian Century, LXXXIII (July 13, 1966), p. 880-81.
King and other rights leaders march in Mississippi after James Meredith is shot.

"Top Man of the Negro 'Revolution.'" U. S. News & World Report, LIV (June 10, 1963), p. 21.
Biographical sketch of King.

Topkins, Sarah B. "Dr. Martin Luther King, Jr." Instructor, LXXX (January, 1971), p. 82.
Poetic tribute to King.

"The Touchiest Target." Newsweek, LXVIII (August 15, 1966), p. 29.
King is stoned by hostile mob in Chicago.

"Tough Years Ahead." Newsweek, LXVI (August 30, 1965), p. 19-20.
King surveys the damage of the Watts riot and speaks of the struggle still to come.

"Toward Peace with Justice in Birmingham." Christian Century, LXXX (April 24, 1963), p. 515.
King continues the rights drive in Birmingham.

"Transcendent Symbol." Time, XCI (April 12, 1968), p. 19-21.
Biographical portrait of King.

"A Tribute to Martin Luther King, Jr." Ebony, XX (December, 1964), p. 126-27.
    Editorial praise of King as he receives the Nobel Peace Prize.

"A Tribute to the Rev. Martin Luther King, Jr." Ebony, XVI (April, 1961), p. 91-92+.
    Top performers pay tribute to King in a benefit concert at Carnegie Hall.

Tucker, Sterling. "Learning Dignity." Childhood Education, XLVI (April, 1970), p. 346-47.
    A tribute to King.

"Two Good Choices." Nation, CXCIX (November 9, 1964), p. 319.
    Editorial support of King's receiving the Nobel Peace Prize.

"Two Perspectives--One Goal." Time, LXXXIV (December 18, 1964), p. 21-22.
    Report of King's being awarded the Nobel Peace Prize.

"Up from Montgomery." Newsweek, LXIV (December 21, 1964), p. 40-41.
    Report of King's being awarded the Nobel Peace Prize.

Vander Zanden, James W. "The Non-violent Resistance Movement Against Segregation." American Journal of Sociology, LXVIII (March, 1963), p. 544-59.
    Discussion of King's use of non-violence in the rights struggle.

"Victory in Jail." Time, LXXXV (February 12, 1965), p. 16-17.
    King is arrested during the Selma campaign.

"Violence Versus Nonviolence." Ebony, XX (April, 1965), p. 168-69.
    Editorial comment on the styles of King and Malcom X.

Wainwright, Loudon. "Martyr of the Sit-ins." Life, XLIX (November 7, 1960), p. 123-24+.
    Discussion of King's activities and his use of the sit-in. This article was reprinted as "Martyr of the Sit-ins." Negro History Bulletin, XXIV (April, 1961), p. 147-51+.

64 / Martin Luther King, Jr.

"Waiting for Miracles." Time, LXXX (August 3, 1962), p. 12-13.
     King and the rights drive in Albany.

Waldman, Louis. "Civil Rights - Yes; Civil Disobediance - No." Louisiana Bar Journal, XIII (February, 1966), p. 229-35.
     A response to King's advocating that unjust laws need not be obeyed.

Walton, Hanes, Jr. "The Political Leadership of Martin Luther King, Jr." Quarterly Review of Higher Education Among Negroes, XXXVI (July, 1968), p. 163-71.
     Analysis of King's leadership and its effectiveness.

Wasserman, Lois D. "Legacy of Martin Luther King, Jr." Negro History Bulletin, XXXVIII (December, 1974), p. 332-33.
     King's legacy is that his memory and his philosophy continue to live.

"When Dr. King Went to Jail Again." U.S. News & World Report, LIII (July 23, 1962), p. 10.
     Reaction by various national leaders to King's arrest in Albany.

"Why They Riot?" National Review, XVII (March 9, 1965), p. 178-80.
     King's sincerity in the use of non-violence is questioned.

"Will This Prophet Be Heard?" America, CXVIII (April 20, 1968), p. 532.
     A plea to fulfill King's dream as a memorial to him.

Willis, Gary. Martin Luther King Is Still on the Case!" Esquire, LXX (August, 1968), p. 98-104+.
     The impact of King's death in Memphis.

Wirmark, Bo. "Non-violent Methods and the American Civil Rights Movement, 1955-1965." Journal of Peace Research, XI (1974), p. 115-32.
     Discussion of the development of the non-violent ideology and King's use of it.

"With a New Weapon." Time, LXX (September 9, 1957), p. 25.

King announces the SCLC will begin to get Negroes to register to vote.

Worsnop, Richard L. "Mass Demonstrations." Editorial Research Reports, August 14, 1963, p. 585-602.
Analysis of King's use of mass demonstrations in Washington, Birmingham, and Albany.

Yevtushenko, Yevgeny. "In Memory of Dr. Martin Luther King, Jr." Negro History Bulletin, XXXI (May, 1968), p. 14.
Poetic tribute to King.

Yglesias, José. "Doctor King's March on Washington, Part II." New York Times Magazine, March 31, 1968, p. 30-31+.
Discussion of King's proposed Poor People's march.

"The Youngest Ever." Time, LXXXIV (October 23, 1964), p. 27.
King is named to receive the Nobel Peace Prize.

"The Youngest Ever." World Affairs, XXX (November, 1964), p. 20.
King is named to receive the Nobel Peace Prize.

OTHER MATERIAL

DISSERTATIONS

Burns, Emmett C., Jr. "Love, Power, and Justice as Central Elements in a View of Social Change: A Comparison and Evaluation of the Thought of Reinhold Niebuhr and Martin Luther King, Jr." Unpublished Ph. D. dissertation, University of Pittsburgh, 1974.
Analysis of the similarities and differences in the thought of King and Niebuhr.

Carpenter, Joseph, Jr. "The Leadership Philosophy of Dr. Martin Luther King, Jr.: Its Educational Implications." Unpublished Ph. D. dissertation, Marquette University, 1970.
King's leadership philosophy and its effect upon

education for a new social order.

Garber, Paul R. "Martin Luther King, Jr. : Theologian and Precursor of Black Theology. " Unpublished Ph. D. dissertation, Florida State University, 1973.
King's impact as a rights leader and as a theologian upon Black America and four intellectual traditions.

Hanigan, James P. "Martin Luther King, Jr. , and the Ethics of Militant Nonviolence. " Unpublished Ph. D. dissertation, Duke University, 1972.
Analysis of the theological and philosophical origins of King's non-violence.

Keele, Lucy A. M. "A Burkeian Analysis of the Rhetoric Strategies of Dr. Martin Luther King, Jr. , 1955-1968. " Unpublished Ph. D. dissertation, University of Oregon, 1972.
Analysis of King's rhetoric to find a difference between King as a minister and King as a rights leader.

Luellen, David E. "Ministers and Martyrs: Malcolm X and Martin Luther King, Jr. " Unpublished Ph. D. dissertation, Ball State University, 1972.
King and Malcolm X are seen as providing Blacks alternative ways of securing the same goals.

Morris, William W. "Strategies for Liberation: A Critical Comparison of Martin Luther King, Jr. , and Albert B. Cleage, Jr. " Unpublished Ph. D. dissertation, Vanderbilt University, 1973.
Analysis of King and Cleage's ideas for obtaining equality and justice and how those ideas were developed.

Rudzka-Ostyn, Brygida I. "The Oratory of Martin Luther King and Malcolm X: A Study in Linguistic Stylistics. " Unpublished Ph. D. dissertation, University of Rochester, 1972.
Discussion of how King and Malcolm X's linguistic styles helped them to express their world views.

Turner, Otis. "Toward an Ethic of Black Liberation Based on the Philosophy of Martin Luther King, Jr. , and Stokely Carmichael's Concept of Black Power. " Unpublished Ph. D. dissertation, Emory University, 1974.
Discussion of the concepts of non-violence and "Black Power"; reasons are given for King's success with non-

violence in the South and his failure with it in the North.

Walton, Hanes, Jr. "The Political Philosophy of Martin Luther King, Jr." Unpublished Ph. D. dissertation, Howard
University, 1967.
Analysis of the development of King's political thought
and how it was influenced by his theological beliefs.

Wasserman, Lois D. "Martin Luther King, Jr. : The Mold-
ing of Nonviolence as a Philosophy and Strategy, 1955-
1963." Unpublished Ph. D. dissertation, Boston University, 1972.
The development of King's philosophy of non-violence
as the method to change existing patterns of segregation
in the South.

White, Clarence, Jr. "Doctor Martin Luther King, Jr.'s
Contributions to Education as a Black Leader (1929-
1968)." Unpublished Ph. D. dissertation, Loyola University of Chicago, 1974.
An investigation of the development of King's theories
and ideologies and how they contributed to education.

Zepp, Ira G., Jr. "The Intellectual Sources of the Ethical
Thought of Martin Luther King, Jr., as Traced in His
Writings with Special Reference to the Beloved Community." Unpublished Ph. D. dissertation, St. Mary's Seminary and University, 1971.
Analysis of the intellectual influences on King's thought
and how they affected his concept of the "Beloved Community."

CONGRESSIONAL RECORD
(In Chronological Order)

United States. Congress. Senate. 87th Cong., 1st sess.,
March 7, 1961. Congressional Record, CVII, 3328-29.
(Also on p. 4490.)
Remarks by Governor Lehman of New York in pre-
senting King an ADA award at the Roosevelt Day Dinner.

____. ____. ____. 87th Cong., 2nd sess., July 11, 1962.
Congressional Record, CVIII, 13275-76.
Remarks by Senators Clark (Pa.) and Javits (N.Y.)
on King's arrest during his campaign in Albany.

68 / Martin Luther King, Jr.

_____. _____. _____. 88th Cong. , 2nd sess. , June 13, 1964.
Congressional Record, CX, 13690-91.
　　　Senator Javits (N. Y.) calls for King's release after
he is jailed in St. Augustine.

_____. _____. House. 89th Cong. , 1st sess. , March 17, 1965.
Congressional Record, CXI, 5307-8.
　　　Criticism of King by Representatives Williams (Miss.)
and Andrews (Ala.).

_____. _____. _____. 89th Cong. , 1st sess. , March 30, 1965.
Congressional Record, CXI, 6333-35.
　　　Representative Dickinson (Ala.) charges King with
Communist affiliations and rights workers in the Selma
campaign with misconduct.

_____. _____. _____. 90th Cong. , 1st sess. , April 5, 1967.
Congressional Record, CXIII, 8497.
　　　Comments by Representative Bingham (N. Y.) criti-
cizing King's anti-war position.

_____. _____. _____. 90th Cong. , 1st sess. , October 4, 1967.
Congressional Record, CXIII, 27814-27.
　　　Discussion of King's career by Representative Ash-
brook (Ohio) attempting to link King to Communism.

_____. _____. _____. 90th Cong. , 2nd sess. , May 16, 1968.
Congressional Record, CXIV, 13736-39.
　　　Reprint of article, "Untold Story of Martin Luther
King, " by John Perilloux that deals with King's alleged
Communist affiliation.

_____. _____. _____. 90th Cong. , 2nd sess. , May 29, 1968.
Congressional Record, CXIV, 15651-56.
　　　Excerpts from Martin Luther King's Three-Pronged
Attack on: I. Christ and the Bible, II. the United
States of America, III. Law and Order, a document
that tries to support King's alleged Communist affiliation.

MANUSCRIPT COLLECTIONS

Alabama State College. Materials relating to Negroes, Ala-
　　bama State College G. W. Trenholm Memorial Library.
　　Material concerning King and his involvement with

the Montgomery boycott and the Selma-Montgomery march.

American Civil Liberties Union. Records, 1948-66, American
Civil Liberties Union Greater Philadelphia Branch.
Material from the ACLU's files on King's work in the
struggle for civil rights.

Butler, Walker. Papers, 1921-69, University of Illinois at
Chicago Circle Library.
Material relating to King's activities for better hous-
ing for Chicago's ghettos.

Highlander Folk School. Tapes and Archives, Tennessee
State Library and Archives.
Material concerning King's role in the rights move-
ment and his attendance at some sessions at Highlander.

Long, Harvey L. Papers, 1919-68, University of Illinois at
Chicago Circle Library.
Contains a copy of King's original Birmingham letter.

McCallister, Frank. Papers, University of Illinois at Chicago Circle Library.
Includes correspondence from Mrs. King thanking
McCallister for gathering information relating to her husband.

North Shore Summer Housing Project Collection. Miscella-
neous items, 1965-66, University of Illinois at Chicago
Circle Library.
Material relating to King's open housing drive in
Chicago.

O'Hara, Barratt. Papers, 1948-68, University of Illinois at
Chicago Circle Library.
Material concerning King and the Selma campaign.

Ralph J. Bunche Oral History Collection. Taped-recorded
interviews, Moorland-Spingarn Research Center Howard
University.
Interviews with hundreds of people involved with the
civil rights movement, including Dr. L. Harold DeWolf,
King's academic advisor while at Boston University. This
collection has been renamed from the Civil Rights Docu-
mentation Project.

Spivak, Lawrence E. Papers, 1927-70. Library of Congress

Manuscript Division.
Contains letters from viewers in reaction to King's appearances on Spivak's "Meet the Press. "

Student Nonviolent Coordinating Committee Collection. Papers, 1960-65, University of Illinois at Chicago Circle Library.
Material relating to King's activities in the rights struggle and his philosophy of non-violence.

III

WORKS THAT INCLUDE KING OR
CONCERN HIS FAMILY, ASSOCIATES,
OR HIS DEATH

MONOGRAPHS

Adams, Russell L. <u>Great Negroes Past and Present</u>. Chicago: Afro-American Publishing Company, 1963.
   Profiles of Negroes who made a significant contribution in various fields of endeavor. A profile of King is included.

Allen, Harold C. <u>Great Black Americans</u>. West Haven, Conn. : Pendulum Press, Inc. , 1971.
   Biographical material on King, Jackie Robinson, Booker T. Washington, and W. E. B. DuBois. The section on King places an emphasis on his use of non-violence.

Allen, Robert L. <u>A Guide to Black Power; An Historical Analysis</u>. London: Victor Gollancz, Ltd. , 1970.
   This overview of the civil rights struggle looks at King in Montgomery, Chicago, and Memphis, though emphasis is placed on the effects of King's leadership on the entire movement.

Alvarez, Joseph A. <u>From Reconstruction to Revolution: The Blacks' Struggle for Equality</u>. New York: Atheneum, 1971.
   This work contains reference to King's leadership in Montgomery, Birmingham, at the Lincoln Memorial, and during the Selma-Montgomery march.

*Banks, James A. <u>March Toward Freedom</u>. Belmont, Calif. : Fearon Publishers, 1970.
   A survey of the struggle for equality. It touches upon the highlights of King's career from the bus boycott to the assassination. King is also mentioned in a section

71

on "Outstanding Black Americans. "

*Bartlett, Robert M. They Stand Invincible; Men Who Are Reshaping Our World. New York: Thomas Y. Crowell Company, 1959.
    King is included in these sketches of contemporary world leaders.

Bell, Inge P. CORE and the Strategy of Nonviolence. New York: Random House, 1968.
    CORE's use of non-violent theories helped lay the foundation for King's later success.

Bennett, Lerone, Jr. Before the Mayflower; A History of Black America, 4th ed. Chicago: Johnson Publishing Company, Inc. , 1969.
    King's campaigns in Montgomery, Birmingham, and Selma mentioned in the section on the modern civil rights movement.

_____. Confrontation Black and White. Chicago: Johnson Publishing Company, Inc. , 1965.
    This study of Black/White confrontations in the U. S. assesses King's impact in Montgomery, Birmingham, Albany, and Selma.

_____. The Negro Mood and Other Essays. Chicago: Johnson Publishing Company, Inc. , 1964.
    The chapter on "Project C" (code name for the Birmingham demonstrations) has references to King.

Bergman, Peter M. The Chronological History of the Negro in America. New York: Harper & Row, Publishers, 1969.
    King's career is traced on a year-by-year basis in section on the civil rights movement.

Berry, Mary F. Black Resistance, White Law; A History of Constitutional Racism in America. New York: Appleton-Century-Crofts, 1971.
    General references to King in his capacity as a civil rights leader.

Birnie, Ian H. Four Working for Humanity; Luther King, Huddleston, Symanowski, and Bonhoeffer. London: Edward Arnold, Ltd. , 1969.
    Biographical sketch of King covers the highlights of

his career.

Black, Edwin. "The 'Vision' of Martin Luther King, " in
Literature as Revolt and Revolt as Literature: Three
Studies in the Rhetoric of Non-Oratorical Forms. Min-
neapolis: University of Minnesota, 1970.
An analysis of King's writings to determine if they
could be considered revolutionary literature.

The Black Man in Search of Power. London: Thomas Nelson and Sons, Ltd. , 1968.
Some analysis of King's leadership in the American
movement for civil rights and how it will be affected by
his death.

Boggs, James. Racism and the Class Struggle: Further
Pages from a Black Worker's Notebook. New York:
Monthly Review Press, 1970.
Some mention of King's importance to the rights
struggle and the ramifications of his death.

Booker, Simeon. Black Man's America. Englewood Cliffs,
N. J. : Prentice-Hall, Inc. , 1964.
King seen as a dominant force in the movement for
civil rights.

Boutelle, Paul, George Novack, Clifton DeBarry, and Joseph
Hansen. Murder in Memphis; Martin Luther King and
the Future of the Black Liberation Struggle. New York:
Merit Publishers, 1968.
An assessment of the impact of King's death upon
the civil rights movement.

Boyd, Malcolm. You Can't Kill the Dream. Richmond, Va. :
John Knox Press, 1968.
Reflections on the deaths of King and the two Ken-
nedys.

Bracey, John H. , August Meier, and Elliott Rudwick, eds.
Conflict and Competition: Studies in the Recent Black
Protest Movement. Belmont, Calif. : Wadsworth Pub-
lishing Company, Inc. , 1971.
King's leadership in the rights movement is studied.

Brink, William, and Louis Harris. Black and White; A Study
of U. S. Racial Attitudes Today. New York: Simon &
Schuster, 1967.

The effects of "Black Power" and the Chicago campaign on King's leadership position are studied.

_____. Negro Revolution in America. New York: Simon & Schuster, 1964.
Some analysis of King's role as civil rights leader and as minister.

Brisbane, Robert H. Black Activism; Racial Revolution in the United States, 1954-1970. Valley Forge, Pa.: Judson Press, 1974.
The gambit of King's work for civil rights is touched upon in this study.

Brooks, Thomas R. Walls Come Tumbling Down: A History of the Civil Rights Movement, 1940-1970. Englewood Cliffs, N.J.: Prentice-Hall, Inc., 1974.
Numerous references to King and his work in the rights struggle.

Broom, Leonard, and Norval D. Glenn, Transformation of the Negro American. New York: Harper & Row, Publishers, 1965.
King cited as part of the new leadership in the rights crusade as a result of his success in Montgomery.

*Brown, Vashti, and Jack Brown. Proudly We Hail. Boston: Houghton Mifflin Company, 1968.
Biographical sketches of famous Blacks including King.

Burns, W. Haywood. The Voices of Negro Protest in America. New York: Oxford University Press, 1963.
A section on King and Montgomery is included.

Butwin, Miriam, and Pat Pirmantgen. Protest II. Minneapolis: Lerner Publications Company, 1972.
Numerous references to King's role in the civil rights movement.

Carlisle, Rodney P. Prologue to Liberation; A History of Black People in America. New York: Appleton-Century-Crofts, 1972.
The bus boycott, the March on Washington, and his position as to "Black Power" are used in citing King as a rights leader.

Caws, Ian. The View from Two Murders. Leicester: New
Broom Private Press, 1972.
Poetic tribute to King and Chê Guevara.

Clark, Mary T. Discrimination Today; Guidelines for Civic
Action. New York: Hobbs, Dorman, & Company, Inc.,
1966.
Emphasis on King's use of non-violent direct action
in Montgomery, Birmingham, Albany, and St. Augustine.

Clark, Thomas D., and Albert D. Kirwan. The South Since
Appomatox; A Century of Regional Change. New York:
Oxford University Press, 1967.
Brief treatment of King and some of his early vic-
tories.

Cleage, Albert B., Jr. The Black Messiah. New York:
Sheed and Ward, 1968.
Includes a chapter in tribute to King and his accom-
plishments in the rights struggle.

Cleaver, Eldridge. Post-Prison Writings and Speeches. New
York: Vintage Press, 1969.
Contains a reprint of Cleaver's "The Death of Martin Luther King: Requiem for Nonviolence," which appeared in Ramparts.

Clemons, Lulamae, Erwin Hollitz, and Gordon Gardner. The
American Negro. New York: McGraw-Hill Book Com-
pany, 1965.
References to King in Montgomery and Birmingham.

Coombs, Norman. The Black Experience in America. New
York: Twayne Publishers, Inc., 1972.
References to King and his major victories.

Crawford, Fred R., Roy Norman, and Leah Dabbs. A Re-
port on Certain Reactions by the Atlanta Public to the
Death of the Reverend Doctor Martin Luther King, Jr.
Atlanta: Emory University Center for Research in
Social Change, 1969.
Analysis of the Atlanta reaction to King's death.

Cruse, Harold. Rebellion or Revolution? New York: William Morrow & Company, Inc., 1968.
King considered as an "establishment" leader of the
rights movement.

Cunningham, George, Jr. The Poor Black People. Ham-
tramck, Mich.: Sherwood Forest Publishers, 1968.
Prepared as a tribute to King, this volume contains
text and pictures of the assassination and funeral.

Curtis, C. J. Contemporary Protestant Thought. New York:
Bruce Publishing Company, 1970.
King and his use of Christian ideals discussed in the
chapter on Negro contributions to theology.

*DaSilva, Benjamin, Milton Finkelstein, and Arlene Loshin.
The Afro-American in United States History. New York:
Globe Book Company, 1969.
Chapter entitled "I Have a Dream" contains biograph-
ical material on King, while other chapters have numer-
ous references to his various rights campaigns.

*Davis, Daniel S. Struggle for Freedom; The History of
Black Americans. New York: Harcourt, Brace, Jovano-
vich, Inc., 1972.
General treatment of King's career.

Davis, Grady D. "A Psychological Application of T. R.
Sarbin's Cognitive Strain Model of Behavior to the Non-
violent Philosophy of Change," in Contemporary Studies
in Social Psychology and Behavior Change, edited by
Joseph L. Philbrick. New York: Selected Academic
Readings, Inc., 1966.
King seen as a "dynamic" exponent of non-violence.

Davis, Jerome. World Leaders I Have Known. New York:
Citadel Press, 1963.
Personal reflections on King and others by this
Christian missionary.

Dennis, R. Ethel. The Black People of America. New Haven, Conn.: Readers Press, Inc., 1970.
Some references to King in the chapter on the civil
rights struggle since 1954.

Dorman, Michael. We Shall Overcome. New York: Delacorte Press, 1964.
Reflections of the author's experiences as a reporter
in Alabama in 1962-63; King in Birmingham.

Drotning, Phillip T., and Wesley W. South. Up from the
Ghetto. New York: Cowles Book Company, Inc., 1970.

Profiles on 14 Black leaders; while there is no profile of King, he is mentioned in the ones on Jesse Jackson and Anna Langford.

Dye, Thomas R. The Politics of Equality. Indianapolis:
Bobbs-Merrill Company, Inc. , 1971.
King's use of non-violence seen as a form of politi-
cal process.

Ebony Pictorial History of Black America. Chicago: Johnson
Publishing Company, 1971. 4 vols.
While all four volumes have some coverage of King,
Volume III (Civil Rights Movement to Black Revolution)
covers the widest range of his career.

Ellison, Mary. Black Experience: American Blacks Since
1865. New York: Harper & Row Publishers, Inc. , 1974.
King's use of non-violence is traced from Montgomery
to his opposition to the war in Vietnam.

*Faber, Harold, and Doris Faber. American Heroes of the
20th Century. New York: Random House, 1967.
Biographical sketch of King and 19 others.

Fager, Charles E. Selma, 1965. New York: Charles
Scribner's Sons, 1974.
Detailed account of one of King's most important
campaigns.

Fax, Elton C. Contemporary Black Leaders. New York:
Dodd, Mead & Company, 1970.
While there's no profile of King, there is one of
his wife, Coretta, and he is mentioned in some of the
other sketches presented.

*Feuerlicht, Roberta S. In Search of Peace: The Story of
Four Americans Who Won the Nobel Peace Prize. New
York: Julian Messner, 1970.
Sketches of King and Theodore Roosevelt, Jane
Addams, and Ralph Bunche.

Flynn, James J. Negroes of Achievement in Modern America. New York: Dodd, Mead & Company, 1970.
Biographical portraits of King and other Black leaders.

Fontaine, William T. Reflections on Segregation, Desegregation, Power and Morals. Springfield, Ill. : Charles

C. Thomas, Publisher, 1967.
Discusses King's use of "moral power" and attempts
to link King with Communism.

Forman, James. The Making of Black Revolutionaries. New
York: The Macmillan Company, 1972.
The author's relationship with King during some of
the major civil rights campaigns.

Franklin, John H. An Illustrated History of Black Americans.
New York: Time-Life Books, 1970.
Text and photos of the highlights of King's career.

*Fulks, Bryan. Black Struggle; A History of the Negro in
America. New York: Delacorte Press, 1969.
Coverage of the major campaigns of King.

Fullinwider, S. P. The Mind and Mood of Black America;
20th Century Thought. Homewood, Ill.: Dorsey Press,
1969.
Studies King's use of non-violence and other religious
ideals in the civil rights struggle.

*Garfinkel, Bernard M. Banners of Courage: The Lives of
14 Heroic Men and Women. New York: Platt & Munk,
1972.
Biographical sketch of King.

Geschwender, James A., ed. The Black Revolt; The Civil
Rights Movement, Ghetto Uprisings, and Separatism.
Englewood Cliffs, N.J.: Prentice-Hall, Inc., 1971.
References to King in essays on the leaders and or-
ganizations of the civil rights movement and the use of
non-violence.

Gilbert, Ben W. Ten Blocks from the White House: Anatomy
of the Washington Riots of 1968. New York: Fredrick
A. Praeger Publishers, 1968.
Washington, D.C., in the aftermath of King's death.

Goldman, Peter. Civil Rights; The Challenge of the Four-
teenth Amendment. New York: Coward, McCann &
Geoghegan, Inc., 1970.
References to King's leadership in the struggle for
equality.

_____. Report from Black America. New York: Simon

& Schuster, 1970.
Discusses the Newsweek poll of 1969 and King's leadership in the rights movement and the effects of his death.

Goldston, Robert. The Negro Revolution. New York: Macmillan Company, 1968.
Chapter on the modern rights struggle deals with King.

*Goodman, Morris C. The Civil War to the Civil Rights War. Vol. II of A Junior History of the American Negro. New York: Fleet Press Corporation, 1970. 2 vols.
Highlights of King's career are mentioned in chapter on the civil rights war.

*Greenfield, Eloise. Rosa Parks. New York: Thomas Y. Crowell Company, 1973.
Reference to King's leadership of the Montgomery bus boycott.

Gregory, Dick, with James R. McGraw. Up from Nigger. New York: Stein & Day, 1976.
Reflections of the author's work in the civil rights movement and his relationship with King.

Griffin, John H. "Martin Luther King," in Thirteen for Christ, edited by Melville Harcourt. New York: Sheed & Ward, Inc., 1963.
King's use of non-violence in Montgomery.

Harding, Vincent. "Religion of Black Power," in The Religious Situation: 1968, edited by Donald R. Cutler. Boston: Beacon Press, 1968.
King's relation with the "Black Power" philosophy.

*Harris, Janet. The Long Freedom Road; The Civil Rights Story. New York: McGraw-Hill Book Company, 1967.
King's campaigns in Montgomery and Birmingham.

Harvey, James C. Black Civil Rights During the Johnson Administration. Jackson: University & College Press of Mississippi, 1973.
Credits King and early rights campaigns in the South with resulting federal legislation.

Haskins, James. Resistance: Profiles in Nonviolence.

Garden City, N. Y. : Doubleday & Company, Inc. , 1970.
A portrait of King is included with other advocates
of nonviolent resistance.

Heacock, Roland T. Understanding the Negro Protest. New
York: Pageant Press, Inc. , 1965.
Analysis of the Black protest movement and its
leadership, including King.

Herbers, John. The Black Dilemma. New York: John Day
Company, 1973.
References to King's use of non-violence in the strug-
gle against injustice.

_____. The Lost Priority; What Happened to the Civil
Rights Movement in America? New York: Funk & Wag-
nalls, 1970.
Discussion of the events of 1965; King in Selma.

Heyer, Robert, ed. Am I a Racist? New York: Association
Press, 1969.
Some analysis of King's rhetoric.

Hodgetts, Colin. We Will Suffer and Die If We Have To.
Valley Forge, Pa. : Judson Press, 1971.
A folk play that weighs the alternatives between violence and separatism as represented by Malcolm X, and
non-violence and integration as represented by King.

Holden, Matthew, Jr. The Politics of the Black Nation. New
York: Chandler Publishing Company, 1973.
King seen as a break from the traditional Black
clergy in the South.

Holloway, Harry. The Politics of the Southern Negro; From
Exclusion to Big City Organization. New York: Random
House, 1969.
King mentioned in a discussion of the Birmingham
situation.

Holmes, Richard. "Ordeal of Martin Luther King, " in Listen,
White Man, I'm Bleeding, edited by Phil Hirsch. New
York: Pyramid Books, 1969.
The story of King's start as a rights leader in the
Montgomery bus boycott.

*Holt, Deloris L. The ABC's of Black History. Los Angeles:

Ward Ritchie Press, 1971.
    Sketches of famous Blacks, including King.

Holt, Len. An Act of Conscience. Boston: Beacon Press,
    1965.
    King's participation in the rights campaign in Danville,
    Va., during the summer of 1963.

Huie, William B. He Slew the Dreamer; My Search with
    James Earl Ray for the Truth About the Murder of Mar-
    tin Luther King. New York: Delacorte Press, 1968.
    King's accused killer tells his story of the assassina-
    tion.

Humphrey, Hubert H. Beyond Civil Rights; A New Day of
    Equality. New York: Random House, 1968.
    Personal reflections and assessment of the rights
    movement and King's impact upon it.

*Jackson, Jesse, and Elaine Landau. Black in America: A
    Fight for Freedom. New York: Julian Messner, 1973.
    King mentioned in section on modern struggle for
    equality.

The James Earl Ray Extradition File; Papers Submitted to
    Great Britain for the Extradition of James Earl Ray to
    Face Trial for the Murder of Martin Luther King, Jr.
    New York: Lemma Publishing Corporation, 1971.
    Compilation of the official documents presented as
    evidence to support Ray's extradition.

Joesten, Joachim. The James Earl Ray Hoax; The Greatest
    Police Fraud Ever. New York: privately published,
    1969.
    Analysis of the events concerning King's assassin-
    ation and Ray's arrest.

_____. Trilogy of Murder. Munich, Germany: pri-
    vately published, 1970. 5 vols.
    Contains the author's James Earl Ray Hoax (see
    above) and his works on the assassinations of the two
    Kennedys.

*Johnston, Johanna. A Special Bravery. New York: Dodd,
    Mead & Company, 1967.
    Biographical profile of King and other Black leaders.

Kelen, Emery. Fifty Voices of the Twentieth Century. New
    York: Lothrop, Lee & Shepard Company, 1970.
    Biographical profile of King and others.

Killian, Lewis M. The Impossible Revolution?; Black Power
    and the American Dream. New York: Random House,
    1968.
    King seen as a new style of leader in the rights
    struggle.

Klumpp, James F. "Nonviolence and Black Power: Civil
    Rights as a Mass Movement," in Current Criticism; Es-
    says from Speaker and Gavel, edited by Robert O. Weiss
    and Bernard L. Brock. Slippery Rock, Pa.: Delta Sig-
    ma Rho-Tau Kappa Alpha, 1971.
    Analysis of King's speech, "Love, Law, and Civil
    Disobedience."

Knight, Janet. Three Assassinations: The Deaths of John
    and Robert Kennedy and Martin Luther King. New York:
    Facts on File, Inc., 1971.
    Discussion of the deaths of King and the Kennedys.

Koch, Thilo. Fighters for a New World. New York: G. P.
    Putnam's Sons, 1969.
    Biographical portraits of King and the two Kennedys.

Konvitz, Milton R. Expanding Liberties; Freedom's Gains
    in Postwar America. New York: Viking Press, 1966.
    References to King's leadership in the civil rights
    movement.

*Ladenburg, Thomas J., and William S. McFeely. The Black
    Man in the Land of Equality. New York: Hayden Book
    Company, Inc., 1969.
    King's major accomplishments are mentioned.

*Leipold, L. Edmond. They Gave Their Lives. Minneapolis:
    T. S. Denison & Company, Inc., 1973.
    Biographical sketch of King and Elijah Lovejoy,
    Abraham Lincoln, George Custer, and John Kennedy.

Lewis, Anthony. Portrait of a Decade; The Second American
    Revolution. New York: Random House, 1964.
    Analysis of King's role in the Montgomery and Bir-
    mingham campaigns.

Lincoln, C. Eric. The Black Church Since Frazier. New
    York: Schocken Books, Inc. , 1974.
    King as a leader in the Black church.

_____. The Blackamericans. New York: Bantam Books,
    Inc. , 1969.
    Reference to King's major victories in the rights
    struggle.

_____. The Negro Pilgrimage in America; The Coming of
    Age of the Blackamericans, rev. ed. New York: Fred-
    rick A. Praeger, Publishers, 1969.
    Reference to King and his most significant campaigns.

_____, and Milton Meltzer, eds. A Pictorial History of
    the Negro in America, 3rd rev. ed. New York: Crown
    Publishers, Inc. , 1968.
    Pictures and text on King's leadership in the struggle
    for equality and justice.

*Liston, Robert A. Violence in America. New York: Julian
    Messner, 1974.
    A look at some of the response to King's use of non-
    violence.

Logan, Rayford W. , and Irving S. Cohen. The American
    Negro; Old World Background and New World Experience.
    Boston: Houghton Mifflin Company, 1967.
    Brief treatment of King in Montgomery, Birmingham,
    and Selma.

Lomax, Louis E. The Negro Revolt. New York: Harper &
    Brothers, Publishers, 1962.
    King's early experiences as a leader of the civil
    rights movement.

Lubell, Samuel, White and Black: Test of a Nation. New
    York: Harper & Row, Publishers, 1964.
    Biographical sketch of King is included.

Lyle, Jack, ed. The Black American and the Press. Los
    Angeles: Ward Ritchie Press, 1968.
    Comparison of the images projected of King and
    "Bull" Conner.

Lyons, Thomas T. Black Leadership in American History.
    Reading, Mass. : Addison-Wesley Publishing Company,
    1971.

Biographical material on King and Booker T. Washington, Marcus Garvey, and W. E. B. DuBois.

Martin Luther King, Jr.; A Selected Bibliography. Washington: District of Columbia Public Library, 1976.
A bibliography of works by and about King held by the D. C. Public Library.

Martin Luther King ... We Remember. Washington: District of Columbia Public Library, 1973.
A bibliography of works by and about King held by the D. C. Public Library.

Marx, Gary T. Protest and Prejudice; A Study of Belief in the Black Community. New York: Harper & Row Publishers, 1967.
Analysis of the effectiveness of King's leadership in different parts of the country.

Mays, Benjamin E. Disturbed About Man. Richmond, Va.: John Knox Press, 1969.
Contains Mays' eulogy delivered at King's funeral.

Meier, August. CORE; A Study in the Civil Rights Movement, 1942-1968. New York: Oxford University Press, 1973.
King's relationship with CORE.

_____. From Plantation to Ghetto; An Interpretive History of American Negroes. New York: Hill and Wang, 1966.
King's use of non-violence in the rights struggle.

_____. "On the Role of Martin Luther King," in Black History; A Reappraisal, edited by Melvin Drimmer. Garden City, N. Y.: Doubleday & Company, Inc., 1968.
Reprint of the author's article for New Politics.

_____, and Elliott Rudwick. Black Protest in the Sixties. Chicago: Quadrangle Books, 1970.
References to King in Birmingham, at the Wash., D. C. march, and his position on "Black Power."

Mencarelli, James, and Steve Severin. Protest; Red Black Brown Experience in America. Grand Rapids, Mich.: William B. Eerdmans Publishing Company, 1975.
King cited as a leader in the Black struggle for equality.

Mendelsohn, Jack. The Martyrs; Sixteen Who Gave Their Lives for Racial Justice. New York: Harper & Row, Publishers, 1966.
King is not one of the 16, although some of the people from the Birmingham and Selma campaigns are, and King is mentioned in relation to them.

Metcalf, George R. Black Profiles. New York: McGraw-Hill Book Company, 1968.
Biographical sketch of King.

*Meyer, Edith P. Champions of the Four Freedoms. Boston: Little, Brown and Company, 1966.
King and his philosophy of non-violence are cited in the section on "Freedom from Fear."

*Miers, Earl S. Black Americans. New York: Grosset & Dunlap, Inc., 1969.
King as leader of the modern rights movement.

Miller, Abie. The Negro and the Great Society. New York: Vantage Press, 1965.
King's career from Montgomery to Selma.

Miller, James A. "The Vision of Martin Luther King, Jr.," in Black Leaders of the Centuries, edited by Okechukwu S. Mezu and Ram Desai. Buffalo, N.Y.: Black Academy Press, Inc., 1970.
Reprint of the author's article in Black Academy Review.

Miller, William R. Nonviolence: A Christian Interpretation. New York: Association Press, 1964.
King's use of non-violence in Montgomery, Albany, and Birmingham.

Mitchell, Glenford E., and William H. Peace, III, eds. The Angry Black South. New York: Corinth Books, 1962.
King's use of non-violence à la Gandhi.

Moellering, Ralph L. Christian Conscience and Negro Emancipation. Philadelphia: Fortress Press, 1965.
King's use of Christian ethics, non-violence, and leadership position of the clergy in the civil rights movement.

Morrow, E. Fredrick. Black Man in the White House. New

York: Macfadden-Bartell Corporation, 1963.
    The first Black Presidential aide writes of the rela-
tionship between King and other Black leaders with the
Eisenhower administration.

Morsbach, Mabel. The Negro in American Life. New York:
    Harcourt, Brace & World, Inc. , 1967.
    King's career from Montgomery to the Meredith
March.

Muse, Benjamin. The American Negro Revolution; From
    Nonviolence to Black Power, 1963-1967. Bloomington:
    Indiana University Press, 1968.
    A study of the Black movement at the highpoint of
King's influence.

_____. Ten Years of Prelude; The Story of Integration
    Since the Supreme Court's 1954 Decision. New York:
    Viking Press, 1964.
    King in the early stages of his career.

*Myers, Rawley. People Who Loved. Vol. I. Notre Dame,
    Ind. : Fides Publishers, Inc. , 1970.
    Profile of King and nine others who led "Christian"
lives.

Parker, Thomas F. Violence in the U. S. , 1956-1971. New
    York: Facts on File, Inc. , 1974. 2 vols.
    Violence King was able to deter and that he couldn't
deter.

Parks, Gordon. Born Black. Philadelphia: J. B. Lippincott
    Company, 1971.
    Reflections on King's relationship with Malcolm X,
and the effects of King's death.

Parsons, Talcott, and Kenneth B. Clark, eds. The Negro
    American. Boston: Houghton Mifflin Company, 1966.
    King's career through his Chicago campaign and op-
position to the Vietnam War.

Peck, James. Freedom Ride. New York: Simon & Schus-
    ter, 1962.
    King's non-violence and its inspiration for the "Free-
dom Riders. "

Persons, Albert C. The True Selma Story. Birmingham:

Esco Publishers, Inc. , 1965.
Attempt to discredit the Selma campaign and link
King to Communism.

Peters, William. The Southern Temper. Garden City, N. Y. :
Doubleday & Company, Inc. , 1959.
King and the Montgomery bus boycott.

Petrie, Paul. The Leader: For Martin Luther King, Jr.
Providence: Hellcoal Press, 1968.
Poetic tribute to King in the aftermath of his death.

Pinkney, Alphonso. Black Americans, 2nd ed. Englewood
Cliffs, N. J. : Prentice-Hall, Inc. , 1975.
Mentions the highlights of King's career.

Ploski, Harry A. , and Roscoe C. Brown, Jr. The Negro
Almanac. New York: Bellwether Publishing Company,
1967.
References to King and his major campaigns.

Powledge, Fred. Black Power, White Resistance; Notes on
the New Civil War. New York: World Publishing Company, 1967.
King's major campaigns of the early 1960's.

Quarles, Benjamin. The Negro in the Making of America,
rev. ed. New York: Collier Books, 1969.
King cited as major leader of civil rights struggle.

*Ray, Jo Anne. American Assassins. Minneapolis: Lerner
Publications Company, 1974.
Profiles of 13 men who killed or attempted to kill
various American leaders; a profile of James Earl Ray
and the King assassination is included.

Reasons, George, and Sam Patrick. They Had a Dream.
Los Angeles: Los Angeles Times Syndicate, 1969.
Biographical sketches of King and other famous
Blacks in U. S. history.

Reitman, Alan, ed. The Pulse of Freedom; American Liber-
ties: 1920-1970. New York: W. W. Norton & Company,
Inc. , 1975.
Reference to King as civil rights leader.

Revolution in Civil Rights, 4th ed. Washington: Congressional

Quarterly Service, 1968.
  Highlights of King's career from Montgomery to his
assassination.

Richardson, Herbert W. "Martin Luther King, Unsung Theologian, " in Representative Men; Cult Heroes of Our Time,
  edited by Theodore L. Gross. New York: The Free
  Press, 1970.
  King as a modern theologian.

Romero, Patricia W. , ed. In Black America; 1968: The
  Year of Awakening. New York: Publishers Company,
  Inc. , 1969.
  Effects of King's assassination.

Rose, Arnold M. , ed. The Negro Protest. Philadelphia:
  American Academy of Political and Social Science, 1965.
  King's role in the early rights campaigns.

Rowan, Carl T. Go South to Sorrow. New York: Random
  House, 1957.
  King and the Montgomery bus boycott.

Rustin, Bayard. Down the Line. Chicago: Quadrangle
  Books, 1971.
  Reflections of Rustin's relationship with King from
various rights campaigns and reprints of some articles
by Rustin concerning King.

_____ . Strategies for Freedom: The Changing Pattern
  of Black Protest. New York: Columbia University
  Press, 1976.
  Reflections on the author's relationship with King
during the Montgomery campaign, the Washington march,
and other campaigns.

*Schechter, Betty. The Peaceable Revolution. Boston:
  Houghton Mifflin Company, 1963.
  Use of non-violence by King, Gandhi, and Thoreau.

Schlesinger, Arthur M. , Jr. A Thousand Days; John F. Kennedy in the White House. Boston: Houghton Mifflin Company, 1965.
  King's relations with the Kennedy administration.

Schuchter, Arnold. White Power/Black Freedom; Planning
  the Future of Urban America. Boston: Beacon Press,

1968.
      Analysis of King's ideas of non-violence, the "beloved
community," and his position on "Black Power."

Scott, Robert L.   "Black Power Bends Martin Luther King,"
      in Current Criticism; Essays from Speaker and Gavel,
      edited by Robert O. Weiss and Bernard L. Brock. Slip-
      pery Rock, Pa.: Delta Sigma Rho-Tau Kappa Alpha,
      1971.
      King's response to the upsurge of "Black Power"
advocates after the Meredith march.

Seigenthaler, John.   A Search for Justice.   Nashville, Tenn.:
      Aurora Publishers, Inc., 1971.
      A study of the trials of James Earl Ray, Sirhan Sir-
han, and Clay Shaw.

Selby, Earl, and Miriam Selby.   Odyssey; Journey Through
      Black America.   New York: G. P. Putnam's Sons, 1971.
      Reflections on King by Andrew Young, Rosa Parks,
and others.

Silberman, Charles E.   Crisis in Black and White.   New
      York: Random House, 1964.
      Reference to King's early victories in the rights
struggle.

Sleeper, C. Freeman.   Black Power and Christian Responsi-
      bility.   New York: Abingdon Press, 1969.
      King's blending of religion and ethics into a policy
of social action and responsibility.

Smith, Arthur L.   Language, Communication, and Rhetoric
      in Black America.   New York: Harper & Row, Pub-
      lishers, 1972.
      Analysis of King's writings and speeches as Black
rhetoric.

_____.   Rhetoric of Black Revolution.   Boston: Allyn and
      Bacon, Inc., 1969.
      Comparison of King's rhetoric and that of "Black
Power" advocates.

Sobel, Lester A.   Civil Rights, 1960-1963.   New York:
      Facts on File, Inc., 1964.
      King in Albany, Birmingham, and the Washington
march.

_____. Civil Rights, 1960-1966. New York: Facts on File, Inc., 1967.
  King's career through the Meredith march.

Soloman, Marvin, comp. Martin Luther King and the Civil Rights Movement. Edwardsville: Southern Illinois University at Edwardsville, 1972.
  A bibliography of works by and about King.

*Spangler, Earl. The Negro in America. Minneapolis: Lerner Publications Company, 1966.
  Biographical sketch of King.

Sparrow, Gerold. The Great Assassins. New York: Arco Publishing Company, Inc., 1968.
  Chapter on James Earl Ray and the King assassination.

Stanfield, J. Edwin. In Memphis: Mirror to America? Atlanta: Southern Regional Council, Inc., 1968.
  The aftermath of King's death in Memphis.

_____. In Memphis: More Than a Garbage Strike. Atlanta: Southern Regional Council, Inc., 1968.
  Background material on the issues that brought King to Memphis.

_____. In Memphis: Tragedy Unaverted. Atlanta: Southern Regional Council, 1968.
  Report on King's last march and the violence that erupted from it.

Stang, Alan. It's Very Simple: The True Story of Civil Rights. Boston: Western Islands Publishers, 1965.
  John Birch Society's version of the civil rights movement, calling King a Communist.

Sterling, Dorothy. Tear Down the Walls: A History of the American Civil Rights Movement. Garden City, N.Y.: Doubleday & Company, Inc., 1968.
  Reference to King's major role in the rights struggle.

*Sterne, Emma G. I Have a Dream. New York: Alfred A. Knopf, 1965.
  References to King in profiles of Rosa Parks, John Lewis, and the Rev. Fred Schuttlesworth.

*Stevenson, Janet. Soldiers in the Civil Rights War; Adventures in Courage. Chicago: Reilly & Lee Books, 1971.
References to King as leader in the modern drive for equality.

Stiehm, Judith. Nonviolent Power; Active and Passive Resistance in America. Lexington, Mass.: D. C. Heath & Company, 1972.
King and his philosophy of non-violence.

*Stratton, Madeline R. Negroes Who Helped Build America. Boston: Ginn and Company, 1966.
Biographical sketch of King.

Synnestvedt, Sigfried. The White Response to Black Emancipation; Second-Class Citizenship in the United States Since Reconstruction. New York: Macmillan Company, 1972.
King's campaigns in Montgomery, Birmingham, and Chicago.

*Taylor, Paula. Coretta King. Chicago: Children's Press, 1975.
[Not examined.]

Thompson, Daniel C. Sociology of the Black Experience. Westport, Conn.: Greenwood Press, 1974.
Cites King and the Montgomery boycott as a turning point in race relations.

Thonssen, Lester, ed. Representative American Speeches: 1967-1968. New York: H. W. Wilson Company, 1968.
Contains a reprint of Benjamin Mays' eulogy to King.

*Thum, Marcella. Exploring Black America; A History and Guide. New York: Atheneum Publishers, 1975.
King and non-violence in the struggle for equality.

Toppin, Edgar A. A Biographical History of Blacks in America Since 1528. New York: David McKay Company, Inc., 1971.
Biographical portrait of King.

* _____ . The Black American in United States History. Boston: Allyn and Bacon, Inc., 1973.
King as a leader of the civil rights movement.

Vander Zanden, James W. Race Relations in Transition;

92 / Martin Luther King, Jr.

The Segregation Crisis in the South. New York: Random
House, 1965.
    King and his philosophy of non-violence.

Vivian, Octavia. Coretta: The Story of Mrs. Martin Luther
    King, Jr. Philadelphia: Fortress Press, 1970.
    Biography of Coretta King, her life with Martin and
    after his death.

Wakefield, Dan. Revolt in the South. New York: Grove
    Press, 1960.
    Role of King and non-violence in the civil rights
    movement.

Washington, Joseph R. , Jr. Black Religion: The Negro and
    Christianity in the United States. Boston: Beacon Press,
    1964.
    The religious foundations of King's non-violence.

_____. The Politics of God. Boston: Beacon Press,
    1967.
    King seen as filling void of Black political leadership.

Watters, Pat. Down to Now: Reflections on the Southern
    Civil Rights Movement. New York: Pantheon Books,
    1971.
    Cites King as the predominant civil rights leader.

_____, and Reese Cleghorn. Climbing Jacob's Ladder:
    The Arrival of Negroes in Southern Politics. New York:
    Harcourt, Brace & World, Inc. , 1967.
    Analysis of King and the Selma campaign.

Webb, Robert N. Leaders of Our Time. Series 2, Vol. II.
    New York: Franklin Watts, Inc. , 1965.
    Biographical portrait of King.

Weisberg, Harold. Frame-Up; The Martin Luther King/James
    Earl Ray Case, Containing Suppressed Evidence. New
    York: Outerbridge & Dienstfrey, 1971.
    Analysis of the controversy surrounding the case of
    King's accused killer.

*Werstein, Irving. A Proud People: Black Americans. New
    York: M. Evans and Company, Inc. , 1970.
    Highpoints of King's life are mentioned.

Whittaker, Charles E. , and William S. Coffin, Jr. Law, Order and Civil Disobedience. Washington: American Enterprise Institute, 1967.
    Discussion on the success or failure of King's use of non-violence in reference to his Chicago campaign.

Williams, Daniel T. , comp. Eight Negro Bibliographies. New York: Kraus Reprint Co. , 1970.
    Bibliography of some of the major works by and about King.

*Wintterle, John, and Richard S. Cramer. Portraits of Nobel Laureates in Peace. New York: Abelard-Schuman, 1971.
    Biographical portrait of King as a Nobel laureate.

Wynn, Daniel W. The Black Protest Movement. New York: Philosophical Library, 1974.
    King and his use of non-violence in the rights movement.

Year's Pictorial History of the American Negro. New York: Year Incorporated, 1965.
    Text and pictures of King in Birmingham and at the Lincoln Memorial.

Yette, Samuel F. The Choice: The Issue of Black Survival in America. New York: G. P. Putnam's Sons, 1971.
    Analysis of some of King's criticism of governmental policy, and the effects of his death upon the civil rights struggle.

Yolen, Will, and Kenneth S. Giniger, eds. Heroes for Our Time. New York: K. S. Giniger Company, Inc. , 1968.
    Biographical portrait of King.

*Young, Margaret B. Black American Leaders. New York: Franklin Watts, Inc. , 1969.
    Reference to King in profiles of Ralph Abernathy, Bayard Rustin, and others.

Zinn, Howard, SNCC; The New Abolitionists, 2nd ed. Boston: Beacon Press, 1965.
    King's relationship with this student organization he helped organize in 1960.

PERIODICAL ARTICLES

Abernathy, Ralph D. "My Last Letter to Martin. " Ebony,
    XXIII (July, 1968), p. 58-61.
    Abernathy's sermon delivered at King's funeral.

"Abernathy's Army. " Economist, CCXXVII (May 11, 1968),
    p. 22.
    Abernathy and the Poor People's march that King was
to lead.

"Act of Sanctity. " Christian Century, LXXXVII (January 14,
    1970), p. 35.
    Editorial support for the creation of a national holi-
day on King's birthday.

Adler, Renata. "Letters from Selma. " New Yorker, XLI
    (April 10, 1965), p. 121-22+.
    A view of King and the Selma march by one of the
participants.

"After Alabama; Negroes' Next Battlegrounds. " U. S. News
    & World Report, LVIII (April 5, 1965), p. 37-38.
    King and other Black leaders discuss future plans for
the civil rights struggle.

"After Birmingham Riots: 'Who Has Gained?'" U. S. News
    & World Report, LIV (June 17, 1963), p. 46-47.
    Question of the gains made by King in the Birming-
ham campaign.

"After the Demonstrations. " Economist, CCXVIII (January 15,
    1966), p. 177-78.
    Status report on the rights movement and King's
plans for demonstrations in Chicago.

Altman, Dennis P. "Whither Civil Rights?" Australian
    Quarterly, XXXIX (September, 1967), p. 76-86.
    King's non-violent approach losing its appeal to the
urban ghetto youth.

"'An American Tragedy'; State Troopers Charge Marching
    Negroes at Selma, Ala. " Newsweek, LXV (March 22,
    1965), p. 18-21.
    King's first attempt to march to Montgomery is
turned back.

"America's 'Few.'" Eastern World, XIX (November, 1965),
  p. 5-6.
    King cited for his anti-war stand.

"America's 100 Most Influential Negroes." Ebony, XVIII
  (September, 1963), p. 228-32.
    King cited as one of the 100.

Anatol, Karl W., and John R. Bittner. "Kennedy on King:
  The Rhetoric of Control." Today's Speech, XVI (September, 1968), p. 31-34.
    Analysis of Robert Kennedy's speech to an Indianapo-
  lis crowd upon learning of the death of King.

"Another Loner?" Economist, CCXXX (March 19, 1969), p.
  48.
    The question of a conspiracy in King's murder.

"Anxious Anniversary." Time, XCIII (April 11, 1969), p. 19.
    No real gains made in the rights struggle since King's
  death.

"April Was Cruelest Month: All That Violence Didn't Have to
  Happen." School Management, XII (November, 1968), p.
  64-65+.
    Question of King's death as the cause of the rioting
  that followed.

Arlen, Michael J. "The Air: Life and Death in the Global
  Village." New Yorker, XLIV (April 13, 1968), p. 157-59.
    Discussion of the media response to King's assassina-
  tion.

"Arrested at Last." Time, XCI (June 14, 1968), p. 23.
    James Earl Ray is arrested in England.

"As Race Riots Spread in North." U.S. News & World Report, LVII (August 17, 1964), p. 34.
    King discusses the potential for violent outbursts in
  Northern ghettos.

"As 200,000 Marched in Washington." U.S. News & World
  Report, LV (September 9, 1963), p. 38-44.
    Report on the Washington march and King's speech.

"The Assassination According to Capote." Time, XCI (May
  10, 1968), p. 65.

Noted author gives his theory about King's assassination.

Atkinson, Carolyn O.   "Coalition Building and Mobilization Against Poverty. " American Behavioral Science, XII (November/December, 1968), p. 48-52.
Discussion of King's idea that resulted in the Poor People's March on Washington after his death.

Auer, Bernard M.   "Letter from the Publisher. " Time, LXXXV (March 19, 1965), p. 21.
Comments concerning Time's coverage of King and the events of the civil rights movement.

Austin, Aleine.   "Behind the Montgomery Boycott. " Monthly Review, VIII (September, 1956), p. 163-67.
Analysis of the bus boycott and King's leadership.

Baldwin, James.   "Malcolm and Martin. " Esquire, LXXVII (April, 1972), p. 94-97.
Reflections on the lives and deaths of King and Malcolm X.

Balfour, Nancy.   "Civil Rights or Civil War in the United States?" World Today, XIX (September, 1963), p. 399-407.
Cites different approaches of King and the NAACP toward gaining integration.

Banyai, Ed.   "Labor and the Negro in Montgomery; A Trade Unionist Evaluates the Boycott. " Socialist Call (August, 1956), p. 6-8.
Analysis of King's role in the bus boycott.

Barrett, George.   "'Jim Crow, He's Real Tired. '" New York Times Magazine (March 3, 1957), p. 11+.
King seen as an example of the "new" Southern Negro.

_____ .   "Montgomery: Testing Ground. " New York Times Magazine (December 16, 1956), p. 8-9+.
King and the bus boycott.

Beardwood, Roger.   "The New Negro Mood. " Fortune, LXXVII (January, 1968), p. 146-51.
Opinion poll shows that Blacks are responsive to King and his methods for gaining equality.

Bennett, Lerone, Jr. "From Booker T. to Martin L. "
    Ebony, XVIII (November, 1962), p. 152-62.
        King credited with moving the rights drive "from the
    courtroom to the streets. "

_____. "The Mood of the Negro. " Ebony, XVIII (July,
    1963), p. 27-30+.
        King and the Birmingham struggle.

"Beyond Rights; The Issue of Human Dignity. " Life, LIV
    (May 24, 1963), p. 4.
        Editorial support of King's non-violent methods in
    Birmingham.

"Bid for Jackpot. " Newsweek, XLIX (June 24, 1957), p. 30.
        King's meeting with Nixon seen as vote-getting move
    by the GOP.

"Big Day--End and a Beginning. " Newsweek, LXII (Septem-
    ber 9, 1963), p. 19-22.
        Report on the Washington march and King's speech.

"Big Hunt for Mystery Killer. " U. S. News & World Report,
    LXIV (April 29, 1968), p. 8+.
        The search for King's killer continues.

"The Big Man Is Martin Luther King, Jr. " Newsweek, LXII
    (July 29, 1963), p. 30-32.
        King tops opinion poll about Black leaders.

"Big Step in Right Direction. " Ebony, XIX (August, 1964),
    p. 90-91.
        King promises to test strength of new law as Presi-
    dent Johnson signs the Civil Rights Act of 1964.

"Biggest Protest March. " Ebony, XIX (November, 1963), p.
    29-31+.
        Report on the Washington march and King's speech.

"The Bill of Rights, 1791-1956. " Nation, CLXXXIII (Decem-
    ber 15, 1956), p. 509.
        Editorial comment in support of King on the first
    anniversary of the bus boycott.

"Billy Graham Advises the Wrong Man. " Christian Century,
    LXXX (May 8, 1963), p. 606.
        Reaction to Graham's statement that King should slow

down the rights drive.

Bims, Hamilton. "A Sculptor Looks at MLK. " Ebony,
XXVIII (April, 1973), p. 95-96+.
Story about Geraldine McCullough's sculpture of King.

_____. "A Southern Activist Goes to the House. " Ebony,
XXVIII (February, 1973), p. 83-86+.
Profile of Andrew Young; his relationship with King.

"Birmingham, U. S. A.: 'Look at Them Run. '" Newsweek,
LXI (May 13, 1963), p. 27-28.
King and the Birmingham campaign.

"Black Belt on the March. " Economist, CCXIV (February
13, 1965), p. 668.
King begins the voter registration drive in Selma.

"Black Hope; White Hope. " Life, LXVII (November 21, 1969),
p. 67-76.
Profile of Jesse Jackson; his relationship with King.

"Black Jacobins. " Economist, CCXV (April 10, 1965), p. 178.
King gets pressure by militants to abandon non-violent philosophy.

"The 'Black Power' Rhubarb. " Nation, CCIII (July 25, 1966),
p. 68.
Editorial about increasing militancy and King's response to it.

"Black Power: Road to Disaster?" Newsweek, LXVIII (August 22, 1966), p. 32+.
Competition to King and other moderates increases
from militant factions.

Bleeckey, Ted. "Communicating: How One Union Did It. "
American Federationist, LXXVII (April, 1970), p. 7.
The American Federation of Teachers develops a
teacher's kit to use researching King's life.

Boeth, Richard. "The March of Time. " Newsweek, LXXXII
(September 10, 1973), p. 24-26.
Reflections on the civil rights movement and the
leaders of the Washington march on the 10th anniversary
of the march.

Booker, Simeon. "America's Most Influential Negro?" Ebony, XVII (February, 1962), p. 31-32+.
King ranked second behind Ralph Bunche.

_____. "As D. C. Burns, President Moves to Head Off Race Confrontation." Jet, XXXIV (April 18, 1968), p. 38-41.
Aftermath of King's assassination in Washington, D. C.

_____. "Returns to Walk in Footsteps of Husband Felled by Assassin." Jet, XXXIV (April 25, 1968), p. 6-16.
Coretta King marching in Memphis and at the funeral.

_____. "Rev. Abernathy 'To Get Moving on Job Left Behind by Martin.'" Jet, XXXIV (April 25, 1968), p. 48-51.
Abernathy left to carry on King's programs.

_____. "Tickertape USA." Jet, XXXIV (April 18, 1968), p. 12-13.
Editorial comment on the effects King's death will have.

Bottone, Sam. "Negro Revolt: The Push Beyond Liberalism." New Politics, III (Summer, 1964), p. 35-53.
Analysis of King and Civil Rights leaders.

Bowles, Chester. "What Negroes Can Learn from Gandhi." Saturday Evening Post, CCXXX (March 1, 1958), p. 19-21+.
Gandhi's philosophy and how King has adapted it for use in the rights struggle.

Boyle, Sarah P., and John H. Griffin. "The Racial Crisis: An Exchange of Letters." Christian Century, LXXXV (May 22, 1968), p. 679-83.
Blacks have moved away from King's brand of protest.

Braden, Anne. "The Southern Freedom Movement in Perspective." Monthly Review, XVII (July/August, 1965), p. 1-93.
Overview of the civil rights movement and King's leadership role within it.

Breitman, George. "How Minority Can Change Society." International Socialist Review, XXV (Spring, 1964), p. 34-41.

Attempt to catch King in a question of the separation of races.

Brodie, Fawn M. "The Political Hero in America: His Fate and His Future." Virginia Quarterly Review, XLVI (Winter, 1970), p. 46-60.
A study of how King, the Kennedys, Lincoln, and others have been treated by biographers and other writers.

Brooks, Gwendolyn. "In Montgomery." Ebony, XXVI (August, 1971), p. 42-48.
Poetic tribute to King in Montgomery.

Brooks, Maxwell R. "The March on Washington in Retrospect." Journal of Human Relations, XII (1st Quarter, 1964), p. 73-87.
King emerges as recognized leader from the Washington march.

Brossard, Chandler. "A Cry from Harlem." Look, XXIX (December 14, 1965), p. 125-28.
A profile of Manchild in the Promised Land author Claude Brown, in which Brown says King and other Negro leaders can't speak for the masses.

Brown, Robert M. "The Race Race." Commonweal, LXXIX (October 11, 1963), p. 73-75.
Comments on the Washington march and King's speech.

Buckley, William F., Jr. "A Memorial for Dr. King." National Review, XXI (October 21, 1969), p. 1078.
Comments on attempts to obtain Federal funding for a memorial to King.

"Bus Boycott Anniversary." Ebony, XXXI (February, 1976), p. 33-35+.
The bus boycott and King's rise to prominence is recalled on the 20th anniversary of the boycott.

Cameron, J. M. "A British View on MLK." Commonweal, LXXXVIII (April 26, 1968), p. 164.
British comments on King's death.

"Camouflaged Killer?" Newsweek, LXXIII (March 17, 1969), p. 37-38.
Ray's trial leaves many questions unanswered in King's death.

"Camping-In for a Dream." Economist, CCXXVII (May 25, 1968), p. 37-38.
   King's dream lives on with the Poor People's campaign.

Campion, Donald R. "Sacrifice for Dignity: Students Protest." America, CIII (May 21, 1960), p. 284-85.
   King's philosophy put to the test in Greensboro, N. C.

Capouya, Emile. "Documents of the Struggle for Public Decency." Saturday Review, XLVII (July 25, 1964), p. 13+.
   King's book, Why We Can't Wait, is listed.

Carberg, Warren. "The Story Behind the Victory." Bostonia, (Spring, 1957), p. 7.
   [Not examined.]

"Carmichael's News Conference--Inciting to Violence?" U. S. News & World Report, LXIV (April 22, 1968), p. 49-50.
   Carmichael blames "White America" for King's death.

"Case Not Closed." Nation, CCVIII (March 24, 1969), p. 356-57.
   Ray's guilty plea leaves unanswered questions about King's death.

Cater, Douglass. "Beyond Tokenism." Reporter, XXIX (October 10, 1963), p. 27-31.
   King as an example of the "new Negro."

"Celebrities Rally to Civil Rights Call by Helping to Raise Thousands in Cash." Ebony, XVIII (October, 1963), p. 120-22.
   King at fund-raising rally in Los Angeles.

"Changing Order." Newsweek, LXI (June 3, 1963), p. 19-20.
   King foresees more activity in Birmingham as new mayor takes office.

Chastain, Wayne, Jr. "The Assassination of the Reverend Martin Luther King, Jr., and Possible Links with the Kennedy Murders." Computers & People, XXIII (February-December, 1974), passim.
   Analysis of the conspiracy theory.

"Checklists of Change; The Civil Rights Drive: 1954-1968." Senior Scholastic, XCIII (September 20, 1968), p. 8-9.

Profile of King and other rights leaders.

"Children of Tragedy: Yolanda King. " Good Housekeeping,
CLXXIV (February, 1972), p. 95.
Profile of the eldest King child.

"Churning Conflict. " Newsweek, XLIX (March 18, 1957), p.
35-36.
Former Communist tries to link King to Communism.

"Cities in '68. " New Republic, CLVII (December 16, 1967),
p. 5-7.
Editorial comment on what to expect from King's proposed march on Washington.

"A City Cracks Down on Demonstrations. " U. S. News &
World Report, LXI (August 29, 1966), p. 10.
Chicago tries to quell disturbances during King's
housing drive in that city.

"Civil Rights Forecast: Maybe a Bit Cooler. " Business
Week (June 4, 1966), p. 31-32.
King warns of potential riot conditions in urban
ghettos.

"Civil Rights Movement Enters Period of Violence. " Congressional Quarterly Weekly Report, XXVIII (November
27, 1970), p. 2863-66.
King's death seen as beginning era of violence.

"Civil Rights Push. " Part I. Senior Scholastic, XCIII (January 10, 1969), p. 12-14.
King's role in the rights movement.

_____. Part II. Senior Scholastic, XCIV (February 7,
1969), p. 8-10.
Reflections on King's death.

"Classic Nobility. " Vogue, CLIII (May, 1969), p. 168-69.
Portrait of Coretta King.

Cleaver, Eldridge. "The Death of Martin Luther King:
Requiem for Nonviolence. " Ramparts, VI (May, 1968),
p. 48-49.
Sees King's death as an opportunity to abandon a
policy of non-violence.

Cleghorn, Reese. "The Angels Are White; Who Pays the Bills for Civil Rights?" New Republic, CXLIX (August 17, 1963), p. 12-14.
King's role in obtaining funds for rights movement.

_____. "Epilogue in Albany; Were the Mass Marches Worthwhile?" New Republic, CXLIX (July 20, 1963), p. 15-18.
Reflections on King's campaign in Albany.

Coburn, Judy. "Open City." New Republic, CLV (September 17, 1966), p. 9-10.
Report on King's open housing campaign in Chicago.

"'Come by Here, My Lord.'" Newsweek, LXIV (November 30, 1964), p. 94.
Coretta reflects upon her life with Martin at her concert in New York's Town Hall.

"Communists and Civil Rights--How Closely Linked?" U. S. News & World Report, LIX (July 12, 1965), p. 12.
Report on accusations that King is a Communist.

"The Continuing Confrontation." Time, LXXXV (April 9, 1965), p. 23-25.
Report on King's proposed economic boycott of Alabama.

Cort, David. "The Voices of Birmingham." Nation, CXCVII (July 27, 1963), p. 46-48.
Excerpts from tapes of King, "Bull" Connor, and others.

Cousins, Norman. "Black Wind Rising." Saturday Review, XLVII (May 30, 1964), p. 22.
Editorial urging Black leaders including King to strengthen their position against militancy.

Cowan, Wayne. "Selma at First Hand." Christianity and Crisis, XXV (April 5, 1965), p. 67-69.
King's role in the Selma campaign as viewed by one of the participants.

"The Crackdown." Nation, CCI (October 11, 1965), p. 205-06.
Editorial about people opposed to the war; King included.

Crawford, Kenneth. "The Non-debate." Newsweek, LXIX
   (April 17, 1967), p. 46.
      Editorial comment about King's anti-war position.

Dabney, Virginius. "The Pace Is Important." Virginia
   Quarterly Review, XLI (Spring, 1965), p. 176-91.
      Comments on King's desire for immediate action in
   the rights drive.

"Days of Violence in the South." Newsweek, LVII (May 29,
   1961), p. 21-22.
      King in Montgomery to defend position of the Free-
   dom Riders.

"Dealing the Negro In." Business Week (May 4, 1968), p.
   64-68.
      King's successors must make a choice about the use
   of non-violent methods.

"Death of a Childhood Friend." Michigan Education Journal,
   XLV (May, 1968), p. 18.
      Effect of King's death on Cornelia Jackson.

"Decision on Bus Segregation." America, XCVI (December
   15, 1956), p. 315.
      Report on King's legal victory in the bus boycott.

"The Deepening Mystery of Dr. King's Assassination." U.S.
   News & World Report, LXIV (May 27, 1968), p. 10.
      King's killer remains at liberty.

"Delicate Balance; What's Ahead for the Negro?" Newsweek,
   LXVIII (November 28, 1966), p. 30-31.
      King and other rights leaders discuss future direction
   of the movement.

"Detroit Feels Brunt of Negro Pressure." Business Week
   (June 23, 1963), p. 90-91.
      King leads demonstration in Detroit.

"Did a Phone Call Elect Kennedy President?" Negro Digest,
   XI (November, 1961), p. 45-49.
      Analysis of the impact of John Kennedy's call to Mrs.
   King while her husband was in jail.

"Did James Earl Ray Slay the Dreamer Alone?" Writer's
   Digest, LIV (September, 1974), p. 20-21.

Ray's efforts to obtain a new trial in relation to
William Huie's book, He Slew the Dreamer.

"Did Ray Kill King?" Senior Scholastic, XCIII (November 15,
1968), p. 8.
Ray's trail begins in Memphis.

"Did You Kill Dr. King?" Time, XCII (July 5, 1968), p. 22.
Ray's fight against extradition.

Dienstfrey, Ted. "A Conference on the Sit-ins." Commentary, XXIX (June, 1960), p. 524-28.
King at a SCLC conference on sit-ins.

"Direct Action in the South." New South, XVIII (October/
November, 1963), p. 1-32.
King's leadership of the rights struggle in the early
60's.

"'A Dirty Business.'" Nation, CCVIII (June 23, 1969), p.
780-81.
Report on the FBI's wiretap of King.

"Disclose the Evidence." Nation, CCXXI (December 13,
1975), p. 611-12.
Editorial seeking an investigation of CIA and FBI
activity in the King and JFK assassination investigations.

Dixon, John R. "Poetry Honors Dr. Martin Luther King."
Elementary English, LII (January, 1975), p. 108.
Poetic tribute to King in honor of his birthday by
Buffalo school children.

"Dr. Herberg Replies." National Review, XVI (September 8,
1964), p. 784.
Herberg defends his position from an earlier article
concerning early Christian demonstrators and their rele-
vance to King.

"Dr. King: A Year Later." Nation, CCVIII (April 14, 1969),
p. 453.
Report of some of the occurrences on the first anniversary of King's death.

"Dr. King's Legacy." Commonweal, LXXXVIII (April 19,
1968), p. 125-26.
King's death calls for a stronger commitment to the

principles for which he lived.

"Dr. King's Murder: Nagging Questions Remain. " U. S.
News & World Report, LXVI (March 24, 1969), p. 13.
     Ray's guilty plea leaves unanswered questions about
King's death.

"A Dream--Still Unfulfilled. " Newsweek, LXXIII (April 14,
1969), p. 34-35.
     A status report on the civil rights movement a year
after King's death.

Dunne, George H. "This Was Montgomery. " America, CXII
(May 8, 1965), p. 660-661.
     King and the Montgomery situation.

Dykeman, Wilma, and James Stokely. "Montgomery Morning. "
Nation, CLXXXIV (January 5, 1957), p. 11-14.
     King's reaction to the victory in the bus boycott.

"Early Christian Demonstrators. " National Review, XVI (September 8, 1964), p. 783-84.
     Letters in support of King against earlier article by
Will Herberg.

Ellison, Louise. "Cities Aflame ... Young Imaginations on
Fire. " Young Children, XXIII (May, 1968), p. 261-64.
     A teacher tells her four-year-old students of King's
death.

"Emancipation II. " America, CVIII (June 1, 1963), p. 790.
     The split in Black leadership between King and Mal-
colm X.

"The Emergence of James Earl Ray Alias Eric Starvo Galt. "
Life, LXIV (April 26, 1968), p. 42B.
     Suspect in King's murder gets a name and a face.

Emerson, William A. , Jr. "Alabama ... Why Race Relations Could Grow Even Worse. " Newsweek, XLVII
(March 5, 1956), p. 25.
     King says the boycott is a protest for rights.

"The End of Fear. " New Republic, CXLVIII (May 18, 1963),
p. 1+.
     King and the Birmingham campaign.

"Esquire's 5th Annual Dubious Achievement Awards, 1965;
    Jewish Mothers of the Year. " Esquire, LXV (January,
    1966), p. 78.
        King cited for his anti-war views.

"'Even in the Darkness.... '" Christian Century, LXXXV
    (April 17, 1968), p. 477.
        Prayer delivered by the president of Andover New-
ton Theological School at memorial service for King.

"Eulogy Puts Blame for King's Death on American People. "
    Jet, XXXIV (April 25, 1968), p. 17.
        Excerpts from Benjamin Mays' eulogy to King.

Fey, Harold E.   "Revolution Without Hatred. " Christian
    Century, LXXX (September 11, 1963), p. 1094-95.
        Editorial comment on King's part in the Washington
march.

"A First Memorial. " Nation, CCVI (April 22, 1968), p. 522-
    23.
        Editorial supporting gun control legislation as memor-
ial to King and JFK.

[Flanner, Janet.] "Letter from Paris, " by Genet. New
    Yorker, XLIV (April 27, 1968), p. 150.
        Report on memorial service for King in Paris.

Foreman, Percy. "Against Conspiracy. " Look, XXXIII
    (April 15, 1969), p. 112.
        Ray's second attorney gives his reasons why he feels
Ray acted alone in King's assassination.

Frazier, Thomas R.   "An Analysis of Non-violent Coercion
    as Used by the Sit-in Movement. " Phylon, XXIX (Spring,
    1968), p. 27-40.
        Analysis of King's interpretation and use of Gandhi's
philosophy.

"'Freedom Riders' Force a Test ... State Laws or U. S. Law
    in Segregated South?" Newsweek, LVII (June 5, 1961),
    p. 18-20.
        King urges tests of recent court decisions.

"From Birmingham. " Reporter, XXVIII (May 23, 1963), p.
    12.
        Report on King's organizing an economic boycott of
Alabama.

108 / Martin Luther King, Jr.

Fuller, Helen. "Southern Students Take Over." New Republic, CXLII (May 2, 1960), p. 14-16.
King, the SCLC, and student groups seen assuming leadership of the southern rights struggle.

_____. "'We Are So Very Happy.'" New Republic, CXLII (April 25, 1960), p. 13-16.
The sit-in campaign seen as part of King's non-violent philosophy.

_____. "We, the People of Alabama...." New Republic, CXLIV (June 5, 1961), p. 21-13.
King rallys Freedom Riders in Montgomery.

"Gamble in the Ghetto." Newsweek, LXVII (January 31, 1966), p. 24-25.
King's housing drive in the slums of Chicago.

Garber, Paul R. "Too Much Taming of Martin Luther King?" Christian Century, XCI (June 5, 1974), p. 616.
Suggests there's much to be done in the study of King's thinking.

Geller, Evelyn. "Homage to King." School Library Journal, XCIII (May 15, 1968), p. 17-18.
Editorial calling for community involvement in Black areas as tribute to King.

"Georgians Help King Stabber." Christian Century, LXXV (October 8, 1968), p. 1133.
Fund started to aid King's assailant.

Geschwender, James A. "Changing Role of Violence in the Black Revolt." Sociological Symposium, IX (Spring, 1973), p. 1-15.
King's non-violent strategy in changing times.

Gessell, John M. "Memphis in Holy Week." Christian Century, LXXXV (May 8, 1968), p. 619-20.
Report on memorial events in Memphis.

Golden, Harry. "Harry Golden." Nation, CCVI (April 29, 1968), p. 572.
Author learns of King's death while debating Senator Strom Thurmond.

Good, Paul. "Beyond the Bridge." Reporter, XXXII (April

8, 1965), p. 23-26.
  King and the Selma-Montgomery march.

_____. "The Meredith March." New South, XXI (Summer, 1966), p. 2-16.
  King and others join Mississippi march after Meredith is ambushed.

_____. "On the March Again: New York." Nation, CCIV (May 1, 1967), p. 550-53.
  King at anti-war rally in New York.

Goodman, Paul. "The Children of Birmingham." Commentary, XXXVI (September, 1963), p. 242-44.
  King's non-violent strategy in Birmingham.

Gordon, David M. "Communities of Despair and the Civil Rights Movement." Harvard Review, IV (Summer, 1966), p. 49-68.
  King's drive in Chicago seeks socio-economic gains for the Black community.

Goulden, Joseph C. "Gun Barrel Politics." Washingtonian, X (February, 1975), p. 46-52.
  The consequences of the shootings of King, the Kennedys, and George Wallace.

Greenfield, Eloise. "Rosa Parks." Ms., III (August, 1974), p. 71-74.
  King and the start of the bus boycott.

Gutwillig, Robert. "Six Days in Alabama: A Journal by Robert Gutwillig." Mademoiselle, LVII (September, 1963), p. 116-17+.
  Report on one week's activity in Birmingham during King's campaign there.

Halberstam, Michael. "Are You Guilty of Murdering Martin Luther King?" New York Times Magazine (June 9, 1968), p. 27-29+.
  The idea of collective guilt for King's death is rejected.

Hanes, Arthur J. "For Conspiracy." Look, XXXIII (April 15, 1969), p. 104+.
  Ray's first attorney gives his reasons why he feels that King's assassination was a conspiracy.

"The Hard Choice Ahead for 'the Movement.'" Business
  Week, April 13, 1968, p. 30-32.
      The choice between increasing militancy and a con-
  tinuation of King's policies has to be made.

Harding, Vincent. "A Beginning in Birmingham." Reporter,
  XXVIII (June 6, 1963), p. 13-19.
  King and the rights struggle in Birmingham.

_____. "The Black Wedge in America: Struggle, Crisis
  and Hope, 1955-1975." Black Scholar, VII (December,
  1975), p. 28-30+.
  Reference to the highlights of King's career.

Hartnett, Rodney T., and Carol U. Libby. "Agreement with
  Views of Martin Luther King, Jr. Before and After His
  Assassination." Phylon, XXXIII (Spring, 1972), p. 79-87.
  A study of attitudes toward King by the governing
  boards of various colleges and universities.

Heinz, W. C., and Bard Lindeman. "Meaning of Selma March:
  Great Day at Trickem Fork." Saturday Evening Post,
  CCXXXVIII (May 22, 1965), p. 30.
  King and the Selma marchers as seen by residents
  along the march route.

Hentoff, Nat. "A Peaceful Army." Commonweal, LXXII
  (June 10, 1960), p. 275-78.
  King mobilizes student forces for the civil rights
  crusade.

Hepburn, Dave. "The 'Rat Pack' Gives $50,000 to Reverend
  Martin Luther King." Sepia, IX (April, 1961), p. 42-47.
  Story of a Carnegie Hall concert to benefit King and
  the civil rights movement.

Herberg, Will. "Who Are Guilty Ones?" National Review,
  XVII (September 7, 1965), p. 769-70.
  The author accuses King of setting the environment
  for the Watts riot.

Herron, Shaun. "Southern Negro or Northern Liberal?"
  Christian Century, LXXIII (June 20, 1956), p. 744-46.
  King prepares for his court appearance in Mont-
  gomery.

Higgins, Chester. "Show Biz Stars Loved King, Raised

Funds. " Jet, XXXIV (April 18, 1968), p. 60-63.
Recalls past performances to raise funds for King's campaigns.

Hill, Norman. "Black Protest Turns the Corner." American Federationist, LXXVIII (January, 1971), p. 17-20.
King as civil rights leader.

Hines, Ralph H., and James E. Pierce. "Negro Leadership After the Social Crisis: An Analysis of Leadership Changes in Montgomery, Alabama." Phylon, XXVI (Summer, 1965), p. 162-72.
A study of Black leadership in Montgomery before, during, and after the boycott.

"The Historic Image." Nation, CXCII (June 3, 1961), p. 469.
King cited for presenting an image of democratic leadership.

Hodges, Louis W. "Christian Ethics and Nonviolence." Religion in Life, XXXI (Spring, 1962), p. 228-37.
An explanation of King's non-violent philosophy.

Hofstetter, C. Richard. "Political Disengagement and the Death of Martin Luther King." Public Opinion Quarterly, XXXIII (Summer, 1969), p. 174-79.
Questions whether King's death was the cause of the violence that followed.

"Hot and Cold." Newsweek, LXXI (May 6, 1968), p. 31.
More clues about King's killer.

"Hot and Cool." Newsweek, LXXI (April 22, 1968), p. 24-26.
Reactions to King's death.

"Hotter Fires." Newsweek, LXII (July 1, 1963), p. 19-21.
Reflections on King and his tactics by other Blacks.

Howard, A. E. Dick. "Mr. Justice Black: The Negro Protest Movement and the Rule of Law." Virginia Law Review, LIII (June, 1967), p. 1030-90.
King in Birmingham in a legal context.

Huie, William B. "'I Had Been in Trouble All My Life, in Jail Most of It.'" Look, XXXII (November 12, 1968), p. 96-97+.
Excerpts from Huie's book, He Slew the Dreamer.

_____. "Two Months on the Lam." Esquire, LXXIII
(June, 1970), p. 104-07+.
　　The story of Ray's evasion from capture.

_____. "Why James Earl Ray Murdered Dr. King." Look,
XXXIII (April 15, 1969), p. 102-104+.
　　The author's version of King's assassination.

"'I Like the Word Black.'" Newsweek, LXI (May 6, 1963),
p. 27-28.
　　King and other leaders discuss the direction of the
rights struggle.

"In Changing Times." Time, LXXX (August 10, 1962), p. 14.
　　King commends the Albany, Ga., police.

"The Incredibility of Integration." Christian Century, LXXXV
(November 6, 1968), p. 1391-92.
　　Questions why King's death hasn't brought about any
improvements in the racial situation.

"The Inexorable Process." Time, LXXXI (June 14, 1963), p.
23-24.
　　King and the Birmingham campaign.

"It Looks Like a 'Hot Summer'--With Selma the Beginning."
U. S. News & World Report, LVIII (March 22, 1965), p.
32-33.
　　King's first attempt to march to Montgomery is turned
back.

"'It May Be a Bell Tolling for Me.'" Newsweek, LXXI (April
22, 1968), p. 23-24.
　　Reactions to King's assassination.

Jackson, the Rev. Jesse L. "Completing the Agenda of Dr.
King." Ebony, XXIX (June, 1974), p. 116-18+.
　　King's work is continued by one of his aides.

Jacobs, Paul. "The NAACP's New Direction." New Republic, CXXXV (July 16, 1956), p. 9-11.
　　King and new rights leadership force older organizations to reevaluate their programs.

"James Ray: Manhunt Ends, but Mysteries Remain." U. S.
News & World Report, LXIV (June 24, 1968), p. 34-36.
　　The question of a conspiracy in King's death.

"Jesse Jackson: One Leader Among Many. " Time, XCV (April 6, 1970), p. 14-23.
King's relationship with Jackson.

Jessup, John K. "An Urgent New Reach to Be Equal. " Life, LX (June 3, 1966), p. 88-90+.
King and other rights leaders are discussed with their philosophies for change.

Johnson, Gerald W. "Trial of a Small Town. " New Republic, CXLVI (March 19, 1962), p. 6-7.
King's campaign and his arrest in Albany.

Johnson, Manning. "Wanted--Another Booker T. Washington. " American Mercury, LXXXVII (September, 1958), p. 138-42.
King is rejected as a leader of Washington's stature.

Johnson, Robert E. "How the King Children Remember Their Father. " Ebony, XXVII (April, 1972), p. 75-76.
Profiles of King's four children.

Kahn, Tom. "Why Poor People's Campaign Failed. " Commentary, XLVI (September, 1968), p. 50-55.
Disorganization within the rights movement after King's death.

"Keeper of the Dream. " Newsweek, LXXIII (March 24, 1969), p. 38.
Coretta King works to keep her husband's dream alive.

Kempton, Murry. "All God's Children. " Spectator, CCIX (August 10, 1962), p. 178-79 and (August 17, 1962), p. 206-07.
King and the Albany campaign.

_____. "The March on Washington. " New Republic, CXLIX (September 14, 1963), p. 19-20.
Report on the Washington march and King's speech.

Killens, John O. "Negroes Have a Right to Fight Back. " Saturday Evening Post, CCXXXIX (July 2, 1966), p. 10+.
Questions King's policy of non-violence.

"The King Assassination Revisited. " Time, CVII (January 26, 1976), p. 16-18+.

A reexamination of the evidence in the case of King's death.

"The King 'Conspiracy.'" Newsweek, LXXII (November 11, 1968), p. 92.
The Report on William Huie's efforts to interview Ray.

"King Day." Newsweek, LXXV (January 26, 1970), p. 24-25.
The absence of any national observance to honor King.

"King--From Montgomery to Memphis." Ebony, XXV (April, 1970), p. 172-74+.
King's biography on film.

"King Urges Kennedy to Create Secretary of Integration Post." Jet, XIX (February 23, 1961), p. 6-7.
King seeks Presidential leadership in rights struggle.

"King's Continuing Impact." Christian Century, XC (January 10, 1973), p. 35-36.
Support for a national holiday in King's honor.

"Knives Sharpening." National Review, XVI (December 15, 1964), p. 1094.
Report on J. Edgar Hoover's comments about King.

Kopkind, Andrew. "Civil Rights Split?" New Statesman, LXXII (July 15, 1966), p. 75.
The different positions of various rights groups and their leaders.

_____. "March Against Black Fear." New Statesman, LXXII (July 1, 1966), p. 4-5.
King and the Meredith march.

_____. "New Radicals in Dixie; Those 'Subversive' Civil Rights Workers." New Republic, CLII (April 10, 1965), p. 13-16.
The different rights groups in the South and their leaders.

_____. "Selma; 'Ain't Gonna Let Nobody Turn Me 'Round.'" New Republic, CLII (March 20, 1965), p. 7-9.
King's first attempts to march are turned back.

_____. "A Walk in Alabama." New Republic, CLII (April 3, 1965), p. 7-8.

King on the march to Montgomery.

Krasnow, Erwin G. "Copyrights, Performers' Rights and the March on Civil Rights: Reflections on Martin Luther King, Jr. , Versus Mister Maestro. " Georgetown Law Journal, LIII (Winter, 1965), p. 403-29.
Analysis of King's attempts to get a copyright on his 'I Have a Dream' speech.

Kremen, Bennett. "Night Walk in Harlem. " Nation, CCVI (April 22, 1968), p. 529-35.
Reaction to King's death in Harlem.

Lakritz, Gerda G. "A Choral Reading Observing the Death of Martin Luther King, Jr. " Instructor, LXXVIII (March, 1969), p. 80.
Eulogy to King.

Lee, J. Oscar. "The Freedom Movement and the Ecumenical Movement. " Ecumenical Review, XVII (January, 1965), p. 18-28.
King's non-violent philosophy and its religious background.

Leifermann, Henry P. "'Profession: Concert Singer, Freedom Movement, Lecturer. '" New York Times Magazine (November 26, 1972), p. 42-44+.
Profile of Coretta King; her life with Martin and since his death.

_____. "A Year Later in Memphis. " Nation, CCVIII (March 31, 1969), p. 401-03.
An assessment of the racial situation in Memphis since King's death.

Leonard, George B. , Jr. "The Second Battle of Atlanta. " Look, XXV (April 25, 1961), p. 31-42.
King's arrest in Atlanta.

"Letters to the Editor. " Ebony, XXIII (June, 1968), p. 14+.
Letters expressing sorrow at King's death.

Lewis, Anthony. "Since the Supreme Court Spoke. " New York Times Magazine (May 10, 1964), p. 10-11.
King and the Montgomery boycott.

"Limping Crusade for Negro Rights. " Economist, CCXXIII

(June 3, 1967), p. 1019-20.
Report on the variety of positions held by rights
groups and their leaders.

Lincoln, C. Eric. "Weep for the Living Dead." Christian
Century, LXXXV (May 1, 1968), p. 578.
Memorial editorial urging a continuation of King's
dream.

Lomax, Louis E. "Georgia Boy Goes Home." Harper,
CCXXX (April, 1965), p. 152-59.
Reflections on conditions in the South after meeting
with King.

          . "What Mass Protests Can't Do." Saturday Review,
XLVI (July 6, 1963), p. 11-12.
King's efforts in Birmingham to guarantee justice for
the Negro.

"The Loneliest Road." Time, LXXXVI (August 27, 1965), p.
9-10.
King's statement on the Watts riot.

Long, Margaret. "March on Washington." New South, XVIII
(September, 1963), p. 3-19.
Report on the Washington march and King's speech.

"The 'Long Hot Summer' Begins." Business Week (July 23,
1966), p. 34.
King begins his housing drive in Chicago.

"Long, Hot Summer of Race Trouble Ahead?" U.S. News &
World Report, LX (May 23, 1966), p. 34-38.
Potential for race trouble seen with King in Chicago.

Lytle, Clifford M. "The History of the Civil Rights Bill of
1964." Journal of Negro History, LI (1966), p. 275-96.
King credited with starting the crusade that led to
the passage of the bill.

Mabee, Carleton. "The Crisis in Negro Leadership." Antioch
Review, XXIV (Fall, 1964), p. 365-78.
King represents the minister as a leader.

McClendon, James W., Jr. "Biography as Theology." Cross
Currents, XXI (Fall, 1971), p. 415-31.
Theologians can increase their knowledge by studying

biographies of such people as King and Dag Hammarsk-
jold.

McCombs, Philip A.   "It's So Beautiful to Be Black. "   National Review, XX (April 23, 1968), p. 392-95.
Violence in Washington, D. C. after King's death.

McCord, William M.   "The View from Mississippi. "   New Leader, XLVIII (February 15, 1965), p. 9-11.
Reference to King's advocating a boycott of Missis-
sippi products.

McDonald, Donald.   "The American Dilemma: 1967; An Interview with Gunnar Myrdal. "   Center Magazine, I (No-
vember/December, 1967), p. 30-33.
Myrdal comments about King's philosophy, his anti-
war stand, and other issues.

McGraw, James R.   "An Interview with Andrew J. Young. "
Christianity and Crisis, XXVII (January 22, 1968), p.
324-330.
Young's relationship with King.

McWirter, William A.   "A Character Shaped by a Mean Life. "
Life, LXIV (May 3, 1968), p. 20-29.
Profile of James Earl Ray.

"The Man in Room 5. " Time, XCI (April 12, 1968), p. 21.
Evidence about King's killer begins to accumulate.

"Maneuvers in Memphis. " Time, XCII (October 11, 1968),
p. 61.
Legal tactics in Ray's trial.

"The March--In Step and Out. " Newsweek, LXVIII (July 4,
1966), p. 14-16.
King completes the Meredith march.

"The March Meredith Began. " Newsweek, LXVII (June 20,
1966), p. 27-31.
King and other rights leaders go to Mississippi after
Meredith is ambushed.

"Marching Out the Voters. " Economist, CCXIX (June 18,
1966), p. 1308.
King's marching in Mississippi encourages voting.

"Marching Shoes. " Newsweek, LX (July 30, 1962), p. 15.
King's Albany, Ga. , march is stopped by a court
order.

"Marching Through Alabama. " Economist, CCXIV (March
13, 1965), p. 1134.
King prepares for the Selma-Montgomery march.

"Marching Where?" Reporter, XXXV (July 14, 1966), p. 12+.
Split in rights groups develops while King marches
in Mississippi.

Marshall, Burke. "The Protest Movement and the Law. "
Virginia Law Review, LI (June, 1965), p. 785-803.
Legal questions posed by King in Selma.

"Martin Luther King and the Right to Know. " America, CXX
(March 22, 1969), p. 323.
Ray's guilty plea leaves unanswered questions about
King's death.

"Martin Luther King's Georgia Battle Ground. " Sepia, XI
(October, 1962), p. 36-39.
[Not examined.]

Marx, Gary T. "Religion: Opiate or Inspiration of Civil
Rights Militancy Among Negroes?" American Sociological Review, XXXII (February, 1967), p. 64-72.
Reference to King's blending of religious ideals into
the rights struggle.

Maund, Alfred. "'We Will All Stand Together. '" Nation,
CLXXXII (March 3, 1956), inside cover.
King's leadership in the bus boycott.

Maynard, Robert C. "20 Years After the 'Brown Decision. '"
Current, CLXIV (July/August, 1974), p. 3-10.
Reference to King and the Montgomery campaign.

"Measuring Up. " America, CXVIII (May 4, 1968), p. 624.
Survey of press reaction to King's death.

Mecartney, John M. "Civil Disobedience and Anarchy. " Social Science, XLII (Autumn, 1967), p. 205-12.
Reference to King and his Birmingham jail letter.

Mehta, Ved. "Gandhism Is Not Easily Copied. " New York

Times Magazine, July 9, 1961, p. 8+.
Analysis of King's adaptation of Gandhian philosophy.

Meier, August. "Negro Protest Movements and Organizations. "
Journal of Negro Education, XXXII (Fall, 1963), p. 437-
50.
King and the SCLC challenge the dominant position
of the NAACP in the civil rights movement.

_____. "New Currents in the Civil Rights Movement. "
New Politics, II (Summer, 1963), p. 7-32.
Report on some of King's activities.

"A Memorial to Dr. King. " America, CXXI (October 18,
1969), p. 315.
Discussion of the conflict between the King family
and the Nixon administration over a memorial to King.

"Memphis: An Ugly New Portent. " Newsweek, LXXI (April
8, 1968), p. 33-34.
King's activities in Memphis prior to his death.

"Memphis Blues. " Time, XCI (April 5, 1968), p. 25.
King's march in Memphis turns into a riot.

"The Men Behind Martin Luther King. " Ebony, XX (June,
1965), p. 164-66+.
Profiles of some of King's associates in the SCLC.

Meredith, James H. "Big Changes Are Coming. " Saturday
Evening Post, CCXXXIX (August 13, 1966), p. 23-27.
The author's reflections of his march in Mississippi
and King's participation in it.

Meyer, Philip. "Aftermath of Martyrdom: Negro Militancy
and Martin Luther King. " Public Opinion Quarterly,
XXXIII (Summer, 1969), p. 160-73.
Report of Miami, Fla. , study on the rise of Black
militancy after King's death.

Miller, Loren. "Farewell to Liberals: A Negro View. "
Nation, CXCV (October 20, 1962), p. 235-38.
King says that anyone opposing immediate integration
and full equality is a foe of the Negro cause.

Miller, William R. "Gandhi and King: Trail Blazers in Non-
violence. " Fellowship, XXXV (January, 1969), p. 5-8.

Non-violent concepts and how they were used by
Gandhi and King.

"The Mobilization of Black Strength. " Life, LXV (December
6, 1968), p. 93-106.
Reference to King and his leadership in Montgomery.

"The Moderates' Predicament. " Time, XCI (April 19, 1968),
p. 19.
Who will assume King's leadership role?

"The Montgomery Boycott. " Nation, CLXXXII (February 11,
1956), p. 102.
King's arrest and the bombing of his home.

"Montgomery Spectacle. " America, CXII (April 10, 1965),
p. 474.
King speaks at the conclusion of the Selma-Montgomery march.

"A Monument to a Martyr. " Ebony, XXIX (April, 1974), p.
126-28+.
Report on the King Center for Social Change in Atlanta.

"A Moral Crisis. " Commonweal, LXXVIII (June 28, 1963),
p. 363-64.
Black militancy grows despite King's emphasis on
non-violent methods.

"More Dirty Business. " Nation, CCIX (July 7, 1969), p. 5.
Report on the wiretapping of King by the FBI.

"More Violence and Race War?" U. S. News & World Report,
LXIV (April 15, 1968), p. 31-34.
The effects of King's death.

Morris, Steve. "Birmingham March Strategist Called to Direct King Funeral. " Jet, XXXIV (April 25, 1968), p.
20-23.
King's funeral directed by the Rev. Wyatt T. Walker.

Morrison, Derrick. "Black Liberation Today. " International
Socialist Review, XXXV (October, 1974), p. 24-33.
Reference to King's leadership of the rights struggle.

Muzumdar, Haridas T. "A Comparison of the Civil Dis-

obedience Movement in India Led by Mahatma Gandhi and the Civil Disobedience Movement Led by Rev. Martin Luther King, Jr., and His Followers." Proceedings of the Southwestern Sociological Association, XIX (April, 1969), p. 9-13.
Analysis of the use of non-violence by King and Gandhi.

"NEA President Don Morrison Interviews Mrs. Martin Luther King, Jr." Todays Education, LXI (January, 1972), p. 14-17+.
Coretta King speaks of keeping her husband's dream alive.

"The Nation Surges to Join the Negro on His March." Life, LVIII (March 26, 1965), p. 30-37.
National support for King's drive in Selma.

"The Negro After Watts." Time, LXXXVI (August 27, 1965), p. 16-17.
King's philosophy is rejected in urban ghettos.

"Negro Cry: 'Black Power!'--What Does It Mean?" U.S. News & World Report, LXI (July 11, 1966), p. 52.
King is confronted with the "Black Power" issue.

"Negro Groups Put the Economic Pressure On." Business Week (February 27, 1960), p. 26-28.
King encourages sit-ins and boycotts.

"The Negro in America." Round Table, L (June, 1960), p. 258-63.
Reference to King and his use of non-violence.

"Negro Leaders Ban Demonstrations." Christian Century, LXXXI (August 12, 1964), p. 1005.
King and other rights leaders urge a halt on mass demonstrations until after the Presidential elections.

"Negro Leaders Dividing--The Effect." U.S. News & World Report, LXI (July 18, 1966), p. 31-34.
King and other leaders discuss the "Black Power" issue.

"Negro Leaders Meet LBJ--Here Are the Results They See." U.S. News & World Report, LV (December 16, 1963), p. 48-49.

122 / Martin Luther King, Jr.

Reaction to meeting with President Johnson by King and other Black leaders.

"Negro Leaders--More Militant Now?" U. S. News & World Report, LXIV (April 22, 1968), p. 19-20.
The effect of King's death upon the leadership of the civil rights movement.

"Negro Leaders Warn: More Race Troubles. " U. S. News & World Report, LVI (May 25, 1964), p. 38.
King and others predict an increase of racial violence if civil rights bill is not passed by Congress.

"Negro Tactics: Change Coming. " U. S. News & World Report, LVIII (January 4, 1965), p. 41.
King discusses the rights forecast with other leaders.

"Negro Tries Passive Resistance. " New York Times Magazine, (May 28, 1961), p. 12-13.
King's philosophy put to the test in the South.

"Negroes' Gains. " America, CIV (February 18, 1961), p. 652.
Despite some gains, King gets criticism from right and left wing elements.

"Negroes Go National with Demands for Jobs. " Business Week (August 19, 1967), p. 37-38.
King seeks a better employment situation for Blacks.

"Negroes in America. " Commonweal, LXXIV (April 14, 1961), p. 67-68.
Reference to King as rights leader.

"Negroes Seek Justice in Georgia. " Christian Century, LXXIX (August 8, 1962), p. 954.
King's crusade in Albany.

"Negroes Sharpen Call for Real Equality. " Business Week (November 20, 1965), p. 46.
King impatient with the pace of integration.

"Negroes Tip the Scales. " Economist, CXCVII (November 26, 1960), p. 887-88.
Kennedy's phone call to Mrs. King swings the Negro vote.

Neuhaus, Richard J. "The King Editorial." Commonweal, LXXXVIII (May 31, 1968), p. 315+.
King's historical significance has been overlooked.

_____. "Slur of the Year." Christian Century, LXXXVII (September 16, 1970), p. 1079-80.
Criticism of the view of King expressed in the book The King That God Didn't Save.

"A New Breed--The Militant Negro in the South." Newsweek, LVII (June 5, 1961), p. 21.
A discussion of King and other leaders of the rights movement in the South.

"New Element Is Introduced into Civil Rights Movement." Congressional Quarterly Weekly Reports, XXIV (July 8, 1966), p. 1431.
"Black Power" challenges King's leadership during the Meredith march.

"A New White Backlash?" Saturday Evening Post, CCXXXIX (September 10, 1966), p. 88.
Editorial concerning violent reaction to King's open housing demonstrations in Chicago.

"Newsmakers." Newsweek, LXXVII (May 17, 1971), p. 53.
Ray attempts to escape from prison.

"Night of Terror." Time, LXIX (January 21, 1957), p. 15.
King confers with other leaders in Atlanta.

"Nonviolence on Trial." Economist, CCVII (May 11, 1963), p. 538.
King jailed in Birmingham.

"Notes & Comment." New Yorker, XLII (July 16, 1966), p. 21-25.
Comment about the challenge to King's leadership on the Meredith march.

"Now It's 'Passive Resistance' by Whites--The Albany, Ga., Plan." U. S. News & World Report, LIII (September 3, 1962), p. 43-46.
Albany police try new way to handle King's demonstrations.

"Now--'The Era of Complexities.'" Newsweek, LXV (Feb-

ruary 15, 1965), p. 27-28.
King's actions in Selma point the way toward new
goals for southern rights groups.

O'Conner, John J. "A Famous Letter." Community, XXII
(October, 1963), p. 10.
Comments on King's Birmingham letter.

"Off Hoover's Chest." Newsweek, LXIV (November 30, 1964),
p. 30.
J. Edgar Hoover's press conference concerning his
remarks about King.

O'Leary, Jeremiah. "The Greatest Manhunt in Law Enforce-
ment History." Reader's Digest, XCIII (August, 1968),
p. 63-69.
The search for King's assassin.

"On from Atlanta." Commonweal, LXXVI (July 27, 1962),
p. 411-12.
King comments on the status of the rights movement.

"On the March." Newsweek, LXII (September 2, 1963), p.
17-18+.
Black leaders discuss plans for the Washington
march.

"One Man, One Gun." Economist, CCXXVII (April 13, 1968),
p. 24-25.
Parallels drawn between the killings of King and John
Kennedy.

O'Neil, Paul. "Ray, Sirhan--What Possessed Them?" Life,
LXIV (June 21, 1968), p. 24-35.
Questions about the deaths of King and Robert Ken-
nedy.

Osborne, John. "Dr. King's Memorial." New Republic,
CLXI (October 11, 1969), p. 9-10.
A discussion of the problems involved in obtaining
a national monument for King.

_____. "The Ray Case." New Republic, CLIX (August
31, 1968), p. 11-13.
Thoughts about King's death as Ray's trial starts.

"Other 97 Per Cent." Time, XC (August 11, 1967), p. 12-
17.

Status report on the civil rights movement and its
leaders.

"The Other Side. " Newsweek, LXI (June 10, 1963), p. 29-30.
King receives hospitable reception in Louisville.

Oudes, Bruce J. "The Siege of Cicero. " Nation, CCIV
(March 27, 1967), p. 398-401.
King attempts to integrate a Chicago suburb.

"PW Interview: Gerold Frank. " Publishers' Weekly, CCI
(March 20, 1972), p. 22-23.
Interview with the author of a book about King as-
sassination.

Pagenstecher, Ann. "Martin Luther King, Jr. : An Annotated
Checklist. " Bulletin of Bibliography, XXIV (January-
April, 1966), p. 201-07.
A bibliography of works by and about King.

Parenti, Michael. "White Anxiety and the Negro Revolt. "
New Politics, III (Winter, 1964), p. 35-39.
King does not dispel white fears of Negro "extrem-
ism. "

"Passive Resistance vs. Nonviolence. " Christian Century,
LXXIX (September 5, 1962), p. 1057.
King appeals to all clergy to come to Albany.

Pazicky, Joan F. "Dr. Martin Luther King, Jr. , January
15, 1929. " Instructor, LXXXII (January, 1973), p. 74.
The song "Kumbaya" is adapted to commemorate
King's birthday.

"Peace Prize Causes Controversy. " Christian Century,
LXXXII (January 13, 1965), p. 39.
Atlanta is unsure how to respond to King's award.

Percy, Walker. "A Southern View. " America, XCVII (July
20, 1957), p. 428-29.
Positive view on King and his methods.

"Personalities of 1956: Stars in Their Own Orbits. " Time,
LXIX (January 7, 1957), p. 24.
King and the Montgomery boycott.

"Pertinent Memorials. " Christian Century, LXXXVI (April 2,

126 / Martin Luther King, Jr.

1969), p. 459.
> A summary of various memorials in King's honor.

Pierce, Ponchitta. "The Legacy of Martin Luther King."
McCall's, CI (April, 1974), p. 28+.
> Coretta and the children remember Martin.

"The Pistol on the Steps." Time, LXXXII (October 4, 1963),
p. 38.
> King's statement about proposed Christmas boycott.

Pitcher, Alvin. "Martin Luther King Memorial." Criterion,
VII (Winter, 1968), p. 3-4.
> A fitting memorial to King would be to "insure liberty and justice for all."

Piven, Frances F., and Richard A. Cloward. "Dissensus
Politics; A Strategy for Winning Economic Rights." New
Republic, CLVIII (April 20, 1968), p. 20-24.
> King's methods and their effect on obtaining rights
legislation.

"Plea to the President." New Republic, CXXXVI (February
4, 1957), p. 6.
> King and other rights leaders appeal to Eisenhower
to bring peace to the South.

Plenn, Abel. "Report on Montgomery a Year After." New
York Times Magazine (December 29, 1957), p. 11+.
> The situation in Montgomery a year after the boycott
victory.

"The Poor Close In on Washington." Business Week (May 18,
1968), p. 34-35.
> King's memory is kept alive by the Poor People's
March.

"Posthumous Pillory." Time, XCVI (August 17, 1970), p.
12-13.
> An attempt to counter some of the charges against
King made in the book The King God Didn't Save.

"Prayer Pilgrimage to the Nation's Capital." American Socialist (June, 1957), p. 5-7.
> King speaks at prayer pilgrimage.

"Prayers and Brickbats." Newsweek, LX (August 6, 1962),

p. 19.
    Non-violent demonstration led by King turns to vio-
lence in Albany.

Preece, Harold. "Hatred for Whites and Preachers Led to
    Stabbing of Martin Luther King." Sepia, VII (January,
    1959), p. 52-56.
    [Not examined.]

"The Price of James Earl Ray." Time, XCII (September 13,
    1968), p. 47.
    Ray sells the rights to his biography to William Huie.

"Pro King." Christian Century, LXXXVII (November 11,
    1970), p. 1358.
    Letter supporting King and the position taken by
Richard Neuhaus in article, "Slur of the Year."

"Publishers Rush New Issues of Dr. King's Books." Pub-
    lishers' Weekly, CXCIII (April 15, 1968), p. 73.
    Reaction of the publishing world to King's death.

"The Queen Is with Us." Newsweek, LXXIII (May 12, 1969),
    p. 37.
    Coretta King carries on her husband's work.

"Race Issue Inflamed Again: Aftermath of a Shooting." U.S.
    News & World Report, LX (June 20, 1966), p. 36-38.
    King marches in Mississippi after James Meredith
is ambushed.

"Race Violence in the 'Oldest City.'" U.S. News & World
    Report, LVI (June 22, 1964), p. 8.
    King's integration drive in St. Augustine, Fla.

"The Racial Scene." Christian Century, LXXXIII (July 27,
    1966), p. 930.
    The distribution of recordings of speeches by King
creates a controversy in South Africa.

"Racism in Reverse." Economist, CCXX (July 16, 1966),
    p. 261.
    Confrontation between King and "Black Power" advo-
cates.

"Raising a Whirlwind." Time, XCIII (March 21, 1969), p.

16-17.
Guilty plea by Ray leaves unanswered questions about
King's death.

"Rally and Tragedy. " Senior Scholastic, LXXXVI (April 8,
1965), p. 18-19.
Civil rights worker is killed along King's march
route to Montgomery.

"Rampage and Restraint. " Time, XCI (April 19, 1968), p.
15-17.
Reactions across the country to King's death.

"Rap for Brown?" Economist, CCXXIV (August 26, 1967),
p. 722.
King takes the middle road between extremists and
"Uncle Toms. "

"Ray Admits Killing Dr. King. " Senior Scholastic, XCIV
(March 28, 1969), p. 21.
Comments about Ray's plea of guilty.

"Ray: 99 Years--and a Victory. " Newsweek, LXXIII (March
24, 1969), p. 29-32.
Outcome of the Ray trial and the questions that remain unanswered.

"Ray's Odd Odyssey. " Time, XCI (June 21, 1968), p. 22-23.
James Earl Ray avoids capture for two months.

"Refuses Bond, King May Stay in Jail a Month. " Jet, XIX
(November 3, 1960), p. 5.
King is arrested for trespassing in Atlanta.

Relyea, Harold C. "'Black Power': The Genesis and Future
of a Revolution. " Journal of Human Relations, XVI
(1968), p. 502-13.
King in the middle between radical and conservative
rights groups.

Remington, Robin A. "Moscow, Peking and Black American
Revolution. " Survey (Winter/Spring, 1970), p. 237-52.
Media coverage and comment about King's death in
the USSR and China.

"Request for Reprise. " Time, XCIII (March 28, 1969), p. 16.
Ray attempts to change his guilty plea.

"Resistance Movement Grows in South. " Christian Century, LXXVII (March 16, 1960), p. 308.
King's philosophy used in sit-ins.

"Responsibility and Emotion. " Time, XCI (April 19, 1968), p. 60.
The reaction to and coverage of King's death by the press.

"Rev. King to Debate Sit-ins with Ga. Newsman. " Jet, XIX (November 10, 1960), p. 3.
King participates in televised debate with James H. Gray of Albany.

"The Rev. Martin Luther King, Jr. , in TV Debate. " Jet, XIX (December 1, 1960), p. 66.
King debates Albany newspaper editor.

"The Revolution. " Time, LXXXI (June 7, 1963), p. 17-19.
King brings rights crusade to Chicago.

Rexroth, Kenneth. "The Students Take Over. " Nation, CXCI (July 2, 1960), p. 4-9.
Students employ King's non-violence in sit-ins.

"Riot or Rebellion. " Science News, XCIII (April 20, 1968), p. 373-74.
King's death is a blow to the belief in peaceful change.

"The Riptide of Disunity. " Business Week (April 13, 1968), p. 27-28.
The effects of King's assassination upon the nation.

"Road from Selma--Hope--and Death. " Newsweek, LXV (April 5, 1965), p. 23-27.
Report on King's march to Montgomery.

Rogers, Cornish R. "Martin Luther King and Jesse Jackson: Leaders to Match Mountains. " Christian Century, LXXXIX (January 12, 1972), p. 29.
A comparison of the leadership styles of King and Jackson.

_____. "Martin Luther King and the Bicentennial. " Christian Century, XCII (April 9, 1975), p. 347-48.
The reaffirmation of King's dream as an American Bicentennial celebration.

_____. "SCLC: Rhetoric or Strategy?" Christian Century, LXXXVII (September 2, 1970), p. 1032.
Can the SCLC be effective without King?

_____. "Why We Must Remember King. " Christian Century, XCI (January 23, 1974), p. 59.
Remember King to keep his philosophy alive.

Rose, Stephen C. "Epitaph for an Era. " Christianity and Crisis, XXIII (June 10, 1963), p. 103-110.
King stiffens Black resistance to segregation in Birmingham.

Rothbard, Murry N. "The Negro Revolution. " New Individualist Review, III (Summer, 1963), p. 29-37.
King brings the revolutionary concept of non-violence to the Negro drive for equality.

"Rough Trip by Bus. " Newsweek, XLVIII (November 26, 1956), p. 49.
King's response to the Supreme Court's decision against segregated buses in Montgomery.

"Roundup: Foreign Tribute to Dr. King. " Christian Century, LXXXV (May 8, 1968), p. 629-30.
Reaction to King's death in Kenya, Mexico, Europe, and throughout the world.

Rovere, Richard H. "Letter from Washington. " New Yorker, XXXIX (June 1, 1963), p. 100-4+.
JFK gives tacit approval of King's methods.

Rowland, Stanley, Jr. "Jim Crow in Church. " Nation, CLXXXII (May 19, 1956), p. 426-28.
Montgomery's churches are segregated, though King gets some support from white clergy.

Rowlingson, Donald T. "The Minister's Role as Reconciler. " Religion in Life, XXXV (Winter, 1965-66), p. 57-66.
King credited as a minister who seeks solutions to problems.

Rubin, Hans M. "From a European's Perspective. " Reporter, XXVIII (June 6, 1963), p. 19.
Despite King's leadership, Blacks' goals will be hard to accomplish without resorting to violence.

Rustin, Bayard, "The Manifesto. " <u>New Republic</u>, CLVI
(January 7, 1967), p. 23.
King confronts "Black Power" advocates.

Ryan, Stephen P. "Climate of the South. " <u>America</u>, XCVII
(June 15, 1957), p. 322-24.
King and his methods are unpopular.

"Sammy Davis Tells How Benefit Show for Rev. King Was
Born. " <u>Jet</u>, XIX (January 19, 1961), p. 60-61.
Sammy Davis, Frank Sinatra and others put on a
benefit for King and the rights movement.

Sanderlin, G. "Voice of America, Martin Luther King's
Speech at the August 28 March. " <u>Today's Family</u>,
XXXVIII (November, 1963), p. 11-13.
[Not examined.]

Sanders, Charles L. "'God Meant Us to Be Together' Mrs.
King Says of Marriage. " <u>Jet</u>, XXXIV (April 25, 1968),
p. 40-44.
Coretta King speaks of her life with Martin.

Sellers, James E. "Love, Justice, and the Non-violent
Movement. " <u>Theology Today</u>, XVIII (January, 1962), p.
422-34.
King's use of the non-violent ideology.

"The Selma Campaign. " <u>Commonweal</u>, LXXXI (February 26,
1965), p. 684-85.
King campaigns for voter registration.

"Senator Brooke and Dr. King. " <u>Nation</u>, CCIV (April 10,
1967), p. 452-53.
Senator Brooke supports U. S. Vietnam stand, while
King opposes it.

Senser, Bob. "The Negro Awakening. " <u>Commonweal</u>,
LXXIII (October 21, 1960), p. 90-92.
King gives Blacks a sense of dignity.

"A Separate Path to Equality. " <u>Senior Scholastic</u>, LXV (December 13, 1968), p. 82-89.
A discussion on the approaches taken by Black leaders to achieve equality.

"Shadows in the American Dream. " <u>Senior Scholastic</u>, XCI

(January 18, 1968), p. 19-22.
The rights movement and King's part in it.

Shaw, Byrum. "Are You Sure Who Killed King?" Esquire,
LXXVII (March, 1972), p. 114-19+.
Conspiracy theory of King's death is reexamined.

Shayon, Robert L. "The Missing Dimension." Saturday Review, LI (April 27, 1968), p. 52.
Media coverage of King's death and funeral over-
shadows economic dimensions of the race problem.

"'Shock.'" Life, LXVI (January 10, 1969), p. 30-37.
The deaths of King and Robert Kennedy.

"The Siege of Selma." Nation, CC (February 15, 1965), p.
154+.
King prepares his voter registration campaign.

Silberman, Charles E. "'Beware the Day They Change Their
Minds!'" Fortune, LXXII (November, 1965), p. 150-53+.
King goes to Chicago to appeal to ghetto youth.

Slater, Jack. "Five Years After: The Garbage Workers,
Memphis and Dr. King." Ebony, XXVIII (April, 1973),
p. 46-48+.
The situation in Memphis five years after King's
death.

Smith, Baxter. "FBI Memos Reveal Repression Schemes."
Black Scholar, V (April, 1974), p. 43-48.
A report on possible government complicity in the
deaths of King, Malcolm X, and Fred Hampton.

Smith, Donald H. "Civil Rights: A Problem in Communication." Phylon, XXVII (Winter, 1966), p. 379-87.
King tries to open communication between classes.

_____. "The Rhetoric of Riots." Contemporary Review,
CCXIII (October, 1968), p. 178-84.
King and the rhetoric of non-violence.

Smith, Lillian. "Strange King of Love." Saturday Review,
XLV (October 20, 1962), p. 18-20+.
King's use of non-violence in the rights struggle.

"The Southern 'Establishment.'" Christian Century, LXXXI

(December 30, 1964), p. 1618-21.
A report that Southern Baptist periodicals omitted pictures or mention of King in rights articles.

"Splendid Victory for 'the Concerned.'" Life, LVIII (February 12, 1965), p. 4.
Testimonial dinner in Atlanta for King.

"Splintered Left." Economist, CCXXIV (September 9, 1967), p. 882-83.
King vows not to head a third party in '68 elections.

Sprague, Richard E. "Assassination of Reverend Martin Luther King, Jr., the Role of James Earl Ray, and the Question of Conspiracy." Computers and Automation, XIX (December, 1970), p. 39-44+.
A reexamination of the conspiracy theory of King's assassination.

Stackhouse, Max L. "Christianity in New Formation: Reflections of a White Christian on the Death of Dr. Martin Luther King, Jr." Andover Newton Quarterly, November, 1968, p. 95-111.
King's work for peace and brotherhood should not be forgotten.

_____. "The Ethics of Selma." Commonweal, LXXXII (April 9, 1965), p. 75-77.
Reflections by a participant in King's march.

Stanley, Scott, Jr. "Revolution: The Assault on Selma." American Opinion, VIII (May, 1965), p. 1-10.
King and the Selma drive in a negative light.

"Statue of Liberty." New Yorker, XXXVI (May 28, 1960), p. 26-27.
Pro-King demonstration in New York.

Stencel, Sandra. "Black Americans, 1963-1973." Editorial Research Reports, August 15, 1973, p. 623-44.
Reference to King as a leader in the civil rights movement.

Stern, Fredrick A. "Eleven Hours in Chicago." Nation, CCVI (April 22, 1968), p. 529-35.
The reaction to King's death in Chicago.

Still, Larry A. "A Bus Ride Through Mississippi. " Ebony,
    XVI (August, 1961), p. 21-24+.
        King discusses the objectives of the Freedom Riders.

"The Strange March Through Mississippi. " U. S. News &
    World Report, LX (June 27, 1966), p. 48.
        King and others on the Meredith march.

"Strategy for Sit-ins. " Economist, CXCV (May 7, 1960), p.
    535.
        King sponsors meeting to plan sit-ins.

Strauss, Edna A. "Martin Luther King. " Instructor, LXXIX
    (January, 1970), p. 75.
        A song in memory of King.

"Strike Escalates into a Civil Rights Drive. " Business Week
    (March 30, 1968), p. 40-41.
        King becomes involved in Memphis garbage strike.

"Summit Conference on Race, Religion. " Ebony, XVIII (April,
    1963), p. 43-44+.
        King speaks at the National Conference on Religion
    and Race.

"Surfeit of Surveillance. " Christian Century, LXXXVI (July
    9, 1969), p. 917.
        Editorial on the FBI's wiretap of King.

"'Take Everything You Need, Baby. '" Newsweek, LXXI (April
    15, 1968), p. 31-34.
        National reaction to King's assassination.

"Ten Greats of Black History. " Ebony, XXVII (August, 1972),
    p. 35-38+.
        King cited as one of the ten.

"Ten Most Dramatic Events in Negro History. " Ebony, XVIII
    (September, 1963), p. 28-34+.
        The Montgomery boycott by King is cited.

"The Ten Most Important Blacks in American History. " Ebony,
    XXX (August, 1975), p. 130-34.
        "No person in the entire history of Black America
    made as great an impact on the nation as did Martin Lu-
    ther King, Jr. "

"Tension Growing Over Race Issue." U.S. News & World
Report, LIV (May 20, 1963), p. 37-39.
King claims a victory in Birmingham.

"The Test of Non-violence." Nation, CXCIII (July 29, 1961),
p. 42-43.
King and the Freedom Riders test rulings on inter-
state travel.

"That Memorial." Nation, CCIX (October 13, 1969), p. 367.
Discussion of the delay in creating a national memorial to King.

"That Segregated Hour." Christian Century, LXXV (December
3, 1958), p. 1402.
White ministers oppose King's views.

"'They've Caught Him.'" Newsweek, LXXI (June 17, 1968),
p. 53.
Ray is captured in England.

Thompson, Daniel C. "Civil Rights Leadership; An Opinion
Study." Journal of Negro Education, XXXII (Fall, 1963),
p. 426-36.
Reference to King as a rights leader.

Thompson, Phillip A. "The American Negro Student Revolt."
Contemporary Review, CXCVII (November, 1960), p. 613-
16+.
King musters student forces in rights struggle.

Tierney, Kevin. "The Extradition of James Earl Ray." New
Republic, CLIX (July 13, 1968), p. 9-10.
Ray is returned for trial.

"To Fulfill a Historic Role." Time, LXXXII (July 19, 1963),
p. 18-19.
Mississippi's Governor Barnett labels King a Communist.

"To Mourn in Private Is Not Enough." New York State Education, LV (May, 1968), p. 9.
Editorial urging that King's dream be kept alive.

"Tragedy Bursts Upon the RA." Michigan Education Journal,
XLV (May, 1968), p. 15-17.
Reaction by Michigan educators to the news of King's
assassination.

Trasher, the Rev. Thomas R.   "Alabama's Bus Boycott. "
    Reporter, XIV (March 8, 1956), p. 13-16.
        Report on King and the boycott by a local clergyman.

Travers-Ball, Ian.   "India and the Negro Question. " Amer-
    ica, CIX (July 13, 1963), p. 44-45.
        King's rights leadership as seen in India.

"Trouble, Trouble. " Newsweek, LX (September 10, 1962),
    p. 47.
        King appeals to President Kennedy for help in Al-
    bany, Ga. , rights drive.

"A Troubled Nation Adds Up the Loss. " Business Week
    (April 13, 1968), p. 29.
        The effects of King's death.

Turner, Ed.   "The Big March--August 28, 1963. " Catholic
    Worker, XXX (September, 1963), p. 1-2.
        A report on King and the Washington march.

Turner, William W.   "Some Disturbing Parallels. " Ramparts
    Magazine, VI (June 29, 1968), p. 33-36.
        A comparison of the assassinations of King and John
    Kennedy.   This article was reprinted in Ramparts, VII
    (January 25, 1969), p. 127-31.

"Turning to Militancy?" Business Week (June 15, 1968), p.
    134.
        The murders of King and Robert Kennedy lessen
    chances that non-violent protest will be successful.

"200, 000 Join in Orderly Civil Rights March on Washington. "
    Congressional Quarterly Weekly Report, XXI (August 30,
    1963), p. 1495-96+.
        King and the Washington march.

"U. S. Negroes' Goal: To Set Africa Policy. " U. S. News &
    World Report, LVIII (January 11, 1965), p. 60-61.
        King and others seek U. S. aid for African nations.

"U. S. Race-Riot Outlook for '67--What Negro Leaders Pre-
    dict. " U. S. News & World Report, LXII (May 1, 1967),
    p. 50-51.
        King discusses potential for racial trouble.

"A Universal Effort. " Time, LXXV (May 2, 1960), p. 16.

King supports lunch-counter demonstrations.

"Unrest Grows Among American Negroes." Christian Century,
LXXVII (February 24, 1960), p. 212.
King's non-violent methods find support.

"Unsaintly St. Augustine." Ebony, XIX (August, 1964), p.
92-94+.
King joins drive to integrate St. Augustine.

"Updating Sainthood." Christian Century, LXXXVI (April 30,
1969), p. 606.
Failure to make King a saint is seen as a judgment
on the church.

Vander Zanden, James W. "The Nonviolent Resistance Movement Against Segregation." American Journal of Sociology, LXVIII (March, 1963), p. 544-50.
Analysis of King's philosophy of non-violence

"A Very Important Prisoner." Time, XCII (July 26, 1968),
p. 25.
Ray is returned to Tennessee for trial.

"Violence Obscures Issue in Birmingham." Christian Century,
LXXX (May 15, 1963), p. 636.
Some Blacks resort to violence during King's cam-
paign.

von Eschen, Donald, Jerome Kirk, and Maurice Pinard. "Dis-
integration of the Negro Non-violent Movement." Journal
of Peace Research, 1969, p. 215-34.
King's lack of success in Chicago open housing drive.

Vorspan, Albert. "In St. Augustine." Midstream, X (September, 1964), p. 15-21.
Reflections on King's campaign in St. Augustine by
one of the participants.

Wainwright, Loudon. "Some Uncomfortable Questions." Life,
LXIV (April 26, 1968), p. 26B.
How will the racial situation be effected by King's
death?

Wakefield, Dan. "Eye of the Storm." Nation, CXC (May 7,
1960), p. 396-405.
King breaks the "Uncle Tom" mold.

_____. "Give Us the Vote!" Nation, CLXXXIV (June 1,
1957), p. 477-79.
   King speaks at rights rally at the Lincoln Memorial.

Walton, Norman W.   "The Walking City, A History of the
   Montgomery Boycott, " Part One.   Negro History Bulletin,
   XX (October, 1956), p. 16-20.   Continued: Part Two,
   XX (November, 1956), p. 27-33; Part Three, XX (Feb-
   ruary, 1957), p. 102-04; Part Four, XX (April, 1957),
   p. 147-52+; and Part Five, XXI (January, 1958), p. 75-
   76+.)
   King and the Montgomery bus boycott.

Wander, Philip C.   "The John Birch and Martin Luther King
   Symbols in the Radical Right. " Western Speech, XXXV
   (Winter, 1971), p. 4-14.
   Analysis of King used as a symbol of the struggle
against the international Communist conspiracy.

Warden, Don.   "Walk in Dignity. " Vital Speeches, XXX (July
   1, 1964), p. 572.
   Black leader criticizes King.

Warren, Robert P.   "The Negro Now. " Look, XXIX (March
   23, 1965), p. 23-31.
   Reference to King's leadership of the civil rights
movement.

Watters, Pat.   "Memphis Is Also America. " Nation, CCVI
   (April 22, 1968), p. 529-35.
   Response in Memphis to King's death.

_____. "The Mob Behind the Marchers. " Reporter, XXX
(June 18, 1964), p. 34-35.
   King discusses the line of demarcation between a
peaceful demonstration and a riot.

_____. "The Spring Offense. " Nation, CXCVII (February
3, 1964), p. 117-20.
   King and other leaders discuss plans for 1964 civil
rights drives.

"Waving the Red Flag. " Newsweek, LXV (April 12, 1965),
   p. 30-31.
   Charges that King and rights movement are Communist dominated.

Weaver, Claude. "Martin Luther King at Oslo." Harvard
Journal of Negro Affairs, I (1965), p. 30-32.
Critical analysis of King's Nobel acceptance speech.

Weaver, V. Phillips. "Moral Education and the Study of
United States History." Social Education, XXXIX (January, 1975), p. 36-39.
The benefits of studying King's philosophy.

"The Weaver Case: Negro Views." Newsweek, LIX (March
5, 1962), p. 27.
King comments on Congressional refusal to create a
Department of Urban Affairs.

Wehr, Paul E. "Nonviolence and Differentiation in the Equal
Rights Movement." Sociological Inquiry, XXXVIII (Winter,
1968), p. 65-76.
Analysis of non-violence as practiced by King.

"What the Marchers Really Want." New York Times Magazine (August 25, 1963), p. 7-9+.
King and others discuss goals of the Washington march.

"Whatever Happened to ... the Assassins of Kennedy and
King?" U. S. News & World Report, LXVII (August 18,
1969), p. 10.
A report on the prison lives of the accused assassins.

"Whatever Happened to Mrs. Rosa Parks?" Ebony, XXVI
(August, 1971), p. 180-81.
With her, King began the Montgomery boycott.

"Where Is James Earl Ray?" Newsweek, LXXI (April 29,
1968), p. 21-22.
The search for King's killer continues.

"Where Racial Trouble Keeps Erupting." U. S. News & World
Report, LVII (July 6, 1964), p. 6.
King seeks Federal protection for Rights workers in
St. Augustine.

"Which Way for the Negro?" Newsweek, LXIX (May 15, 1967),
p. 27-28+.
King discusses the future of the civil rights movement.

"White Backlash Whips Up a Roadblock in Chicago." Life,
LXI (August 19, 1966), p. 30-30A.

King's open housing drive in Chicago meets resistance.

"White Folks, Wake Up!" Ebony, XX (May, 1965), p. 170-71.
    Editorial comment on the effects of the Selma-Montgomery march.

"Who Killed King?" Newsweek, LXXI (April 22, 1968), p. 31-33.
    The identity of King's killer is sought.

"Who Killed King?" Time, XCI (April 26, 1968), p. 20-21.
    Suspects are sought in King's killing.

"Who Killed the Dream?" Newsweek, LXXXVI (December 8, 1975), p. 35.
    The investigation of King's death may be reopened.

"Who Won What?" Newsweek, LIX (January 1, 1962), p. 13-14.
    King and the Albany campaign.

"Whoa There, Mr. Herberg." National Review, XVI (August 25, 1964), p. 741-42.
    Letters supporting King in response to an earlier article by Herberg in National Review.

"The Whole Truth." Ebony, XXIV (May, 1969), p. 56-57.
    Editorial comment on Ray's plea of guilty and the questions left unanswered.

"Widening Search." Time, XCI (April 19, 1968), p. 20.
    The search for King's assassin continues.

Widick, B. J. "Labor Meets for Peace." Nation, CCV (November 27, 1967), p. 561-63.
    King makes anti-war address to labor leaders.

"Widow Hopes for Fulfillment of King's Dream." Jet, XXXIV (April 18, 1968), p. 3.
    Coretta King says her husband's spirit will never die.

Williams, John A. "This Is My Country, Too." Holiday, XXXVI (August, 1964), p. 30-33+. (Continued in September, p. 58-59+; and October, p. 4.)
    A cross-country journey ends in Washington during the march and King's speech.

Williams, Robert F.   "Can Negroes Afford to be Pacifists?"
    Liberation, IV (September, 1959), p. 4-7.
        King's non-violent methods are questioned.

Wirth, Richard.   "Memorial. "   Michigan Education Journal,
    XLV (May, 1968), p. 19.
        A memorial tribute to King.

"With but One Voice. "   Nation, CCIV (April 24, 1967), p.
    515-16.
        Editorial comment about reaction to King's anti-
    war position.

"The Woman Behind Martin Luther King. "   Ebony, XIV (Jan-
    uary, 1959), p. 33-38.
        A report on Coretta King and her life with Martin.

Woodbury, Richard.   "Murder Clues: Handprints, a Car
    Chase and a Silly Smile. "   Life, LXIV (April 19, 1968),
    p. 40-40A.
        The search for King's assassin.

Woodward, C. Vann.   "After Watts--Where Is the Negro
    Revolution Headed?"   New York Times Magazine (August
    29, 1965), p. 24-25+.
        Reference to King's voter registration project.

Worsnop, Richard L.   "Racism in America. "   Editorial Re-
    search Reports (May 13, 1964), p. 343-60.
        King makes a statement about the 1964 Civil Rights
    Act.

Wurf, Harold H.   "Roadblocks to Integration. "   Contemporary
    Issues (Winter, 1963), p. 3-5.
        King's philosophy of non-violence is questioned.

"A Year Later: Honors for Dr. King--Violence, Too. "   U. S.
    News & World Report, LXVI (April 14, 1969), p. 8.
        Report of the events of the first anniversary of King's
    death.

"A Year of Homage to Martin Luther King. "   Ebony, XXIV
    (April, 1969), p. 31-34+.
        A list of memorials to King during the first year
    after his death.

"'You're Such a Brave Lady. '"   Newsweek, LXXI (April 22,

142 / Martin Luther King, Jr.

1968), p. 32.
Coretta King and the events following her husband's death.

OTHER MATERIAL

DISSERTATIONS

enedetti, Robert R.   "Ideology and Political Culture: The Civil Rights Movement and the American Creed, 1956-1969. " Unpublished Ph. D. dissertation, University of Pennsylvania, 1975.
The writings of King and seven other rights leaders are analyzed for shifts in ideology.

Blackwelder, Julia K.   "Fundamentalist Reactions to the Civil Rights Movement Since 1954. " Unpublished Ph. D. dissertation, Emory University, 1972.
Reaction to King and the Negro struggle for equality by fundamentalist periodicals.

Harper, Fredrick D.   "Maslow's Concept of Self-Actualization Compared with Personality Characteristics of Selected Black Protesters: Martin Luther King, Jr. , Malcolm X and Fredrick Douglass. " Unpublished Ph. D. dissertation, Florida State University, 1971.
Maslow's concept is applied to King's personality.

House, Secil V.   "The Implications of Dr. Martin Luther King, Jr. 's Work and Philosophy for the Field of Adult Education. " Unpublished Ph. D. dissertation, Indiana University, 1975.
King's application of education concepts is found to be inconsistent with theoretical applications.

Martin, S. Rudolph, Jr.   "A New Mind: Changing Black Consciousness, 1950-1970. " Unpublished Ph. D. dissertation, Washington State University, 1974.
Analysis of the changing of Black consciousness as King and others intensify the struggle for equality.

Marty, William R.   "Recent Negro Protest Thought: Theories of Nonviolence and 'Black Power. '" Unpublished Ph. D.

dissertation, Duke University, 1968.
    Includes a study of King and the development of his philosophy of non-violent direct action.

Oglesby, Enoch H. "Ethical Implications of the Works of Selected Black Theologians: A Critical Analysis. " Unpublished Ph. D. dissertation, Boston University, 1974.
    The impact of King's work as a theologian.

Onwubu, Chukwuemeka. "Black Ideologies and the Sociology of Knowledge: The Public Response to the Protest Thoughts and Teachings of Martin Luther King, Jr. , and Malcolm X. " Unpublished Ph. D. dissertation, Michigan State University, 1975.
    Analysis of the public acceptance of the ideologies of King and Malcolm X and the factors upon which the acceptance was based.

Shelton, Robert L. "Black Revolution: The Definition and Meaning of 'Revolution' in the Writings and Speeches of Selected Nationally Prominent Negro Americans, 1963-1968. " Unpublished Ph. D. dissertation, Boston University, 1970.
    The interpretation of the term "revolution" by King and other Black leaders.

Whitehead, Brady B. , Jr. "Preaching Response to the Death of Martin Luther King, Jr. " Unpublished Ph. D. dissertation, Boston University School of Theology, 1972.
    A comparison of the response to King's death by four separate groups of ministers.

CONGRESSIONAL RECORD
(In Chronological Order)

United States. Congress. Senate. 85th Cong. , 1st sess. , January 9, 1957. Congressional Record, CIII, 367.
    Reference to a threat on King's life in Alabama during remarks by Senator Humphrey (Minn.).

____. ____. House. 87th Cong. , 2nd sess. , August 1, 1962. Congressional Record, CVIII, 15320-21.
    King's rights drive in Albany, Ga. , is mentioned by Representative Ryan (N. Y.).

____. ____. Senate. 88th Cong., 2nd sess., June 12, 1964. Congressional Record, CX, 13642-43.
The Comments by Senator Stennis (Miss.) on King's arrest in St. Augustine.

____. ____. House. 89th Cong., 1st sess., February 15, 1965. Congressional Record, CXI, A625-26.
The Miami American Legion supports J. Edgar Hoover's criticism of King.

____. ____. ____. 89th Cong., 1st sess., April 1, 1965. Congressional Record, CXI, 6768-69.
Comments by Representatives Edwards and Buchanan (Ala.) concerning King's proposed boycott of Alabama.

____. ____. Senate. 89th Cong., 1st sess., May 7, 1965. Congressional Record, CXI, 9870-73.
A reprint of an article by Simeon Booker, "50,000 March on Montgomery," which appeared in Ebony, May, 1965.

____. ____. House. 89th Cong., 1st sess., May 19, 1965. Congressional Record, CXI, 10941-42.
King comments on the challenge to the Mississippi Congressional delegation by the Mississippi Freedom Democratic Party.

____. ____. Senate. 89th Cong., 1st sess., September 13, 1965. Congressional Record, CXI, 23567.
Remarks by Senator Thurmond (S.C.) concerning a meeting of King and Bayard Rustin with UN Ambassador Goldberg.

____. ____. House. 89th Cong., 2nd sess., May 10, 1966. Congressional Record, CXII, 10164-65.
Address by Coretta King to the National Conference on Family Planning, presenting her husband's views on family planning legislation.

____. ____. Senate. 90th Cong., 1st sess., April 27, 1967. Congressional Record, CXIII, 11011.
Senator Mondale (Minn.) comments on King's statement concerning possible Presidential candidates.

____. ____. House. 90th Cong., 1st sess., June 22, 1967. Congressional Record, CXIII, 16939-40.
The Rev. Matthew Winters of Camp Hill, Pa., replies

to King's anti-war sermon.

_____. _____. _____. 90th Cong., 1st sess., July 27, 1967.
Congressional Record, CXIII, 20563.
Reprint of the statement by King and other rights
leaders asking for an end to the rioting. (Also found on
p. A3946-47.)

_____. _____. _____. 90th Cong., 1st sess., August 7, 1967.
Congressional Record, CXIII, 21546-48.
Reference to King in remarks by Representative
Fisher (Tex.) about a link between rioting and the rights
movement.

_____. _____. _____. 90th Cong., 1st sess., December 5,
1967. Congressional Record, CXIII, 35101-2.
Remarks by Representative Waggoner (La.) about
King's proposed Poor People's march.

_____. _____. Senate. 90th Cong., 2nd sess., March 29,
1968. Congressional Record, CXIV, 8263-65.
Remarks by Senators Byrd (W. Va.) and Stennis
(Miss.) about the riot in Memphis after King's march
there and the impending march on Washington.

_____. _____. House. 90th Cong., 2nd sess., April 1, 1968.
Congressional Record, CXIV, 8380-81.
Representatives Kuykendall and Everett (Tenn.) comment on the trouble in Memphis and King's presence
there.

_____. _____. _____. 90th Cong., 2nd sess., April 3, 1968.
Congressional Record, CXIV, 8822.
Representative Kornegay (N.C.) urges King to call off
the march on Washington.

_____. _____. _____. 90th Cong., 2nd sess., April 8, 1968.
Congressional Record, CXIV, 9164-66.
Members of the House comment on King's death.

_____. _____. Senate. 90th Cong., 2nd sess., April 8, 1968.
Congressional Record, CXIV, 9227.
Senator Brooke (Mass.) introduces a resolution to
make January 15 "Martin Luther King Day."

_____. _____. _____. 90th Cong., 2nd sess., April 10, 1968.
Congressional Record, CXIV, 9446-48.

Excerpts from statements and prayers delivered at King's funeral.

_____. _____. House. 90th Cong., 2nd sess., April 11, 1968. Congressional Record, CXIV, 9796-97.
Mrs. Robert J. Stuart, president of the League of Women Voters, comments on King's death.

_____. _____. _____. 90th Cong., 2nd sess., April 11, 1968. Congressional Record, CXIV, 9815.
Statement by the California Farmer-Consumer Information Committee honoring King.

_____. _____. Senate. 90th Cong., 2nd sess., April 17, 1968. Congressional Record, CXIV, 9924.
Memorial sermon to King delivered by the Rev. Ronald Winters of Floris, Va.

_____. _____. _____. 90th Cong., 2nd sess., April 22, 1968. Congressional Record, CXIV, 10144-45.
Senator Scott (Pa.) introduces legislation to issue commemorative coins to honor King.

_____. _____. House. 90th Cong., 2nd sess., April 22, 1968. Congressional Record, CXIV, 10241.
Memorial sermon to King delivered by the Rev. Rudolph S. Shoultz of Springfield, Ill.

_____. _____. _____. 90th Cong., 2nd sess., April 23, 1968. Congressional Record, CXIV, 10381-82.
Poetic memorial, "Black Thursday, April 4, 1968."

_____. _____. _____. 90th Cong., 2nd sess., April 23, 1968. Congressional Record, CXIV, 10382-83.
Rabbi Nathan Taragin, Bronx, N.Y., delivers a eulogy to King.

_____. _____. _____. 90th Cong., 2nd sess., April 23, 1968. Congressional Record, CXIV, 10396-98.
King is accused of Communist affiliations.

_____. _____. _____. 90th Cong., 2nd sess., April 24, 1968. Congressional Record, CXIV, 10500.
Memorial address by Judge Frank M. Coffin of Maine.

_____. _____. _____. 90th Cong., 2nd sess., April 24, 1968. Congressional Record, CXIV, 10553.

Memorial address by Rabbi Fredric Doppelt of Ft. Wayne, Ind.

____. ____. ____. 90th Cong., 2nd sess., April 25, 1968. Congressional Record, CXIV, 10760.
"Dr. Martin Luther King, Jr.," a memorial poem by Maurice Sapienza.

____. ____. ____. 90th Cong., 2nd sess., April 30, 1968. Congressional Record, CXIV, 11111.
Dr. Robert Strong, Montgomery, Ala., delivers a memorial address to King.

____. ____. ____. 90th Cong., 2nd sess., May 1, 1968. Congressional Record, CXIV, 11379-80.
Representative Nix (Pa.) supports the issuance of a commemorative stamp for King.

____. ____. ____. 90th Cong., 2nd sess., May 6, 1968. Congressional Record, CXIV, 11971.
Poetic memorial, "The Bells of Death Ring Once More," by Leo Lipp.

____. ____. ____. 90th Cong., 2nd sess., May 15, 1968. Congressional Record, CXIV, 13557-58.
Memorial speech delivered by James C. Abbott of Williamsburg, Va.

____. ____. ____. 90th Cong., 2nd sess., May 17, 1968. Congressional Record, CXIV, 13869-71.
Reprint of Life article, "The Story of the Accused Killer of Dr. King."

____. ____. Senate. 90th Cong., 2nd sess., May 21, 1968. Congressional Record, CXIV, 14189.
Senator Scott (Pa.) introduces legislation for the issuance of a commemorative medal in King's honor.

____. ____. House. 90th Cong., 2nd sess., May 21, 1968. Congressional Record, CXIV, 14240-42.
Tribute to King by Indianapolis Mayor Richard G. Lugar.

____. ____. ____. 90th Cong., 2nd sess., May 27, 1968. Congressional Record, CXIV, 15169-72.
Reprint of addresses delivered at King's funeral.

————. ————. ————. 90th Cong., 2nd sess., May 28, 1968.
Congressional Record, CXIV, 15471-75.
    Reprint of American Opinion article by Alan Stang
linking King to Communism.

————. ————. ————. 90th Cong., 2nd sess., June 12, 1968.
Congressional Record, CXIV, 17023.
    Remarks by Representative Moorhead (Pa.) in support
of the presentation of a medal to Coretta King.

————. ————. Senate. 90th Cong., 2nd sess., June 13, 1968.
Congressional Record, CXIV, 17108-9.
    Text of speech by Jack Greenburg, "Martin Luther
King, Jr., and the Law."

————. ————. House. 90th Cong., 2nd sess., July 18, 1968.
Congressional Record, CXIV, 22126-29.
    Representative Brown (Ohio) calls for an investigation
of the assassinations of King and Kennedy.

————. ————. Senate. 90th Cong., 2nd sess., August 2,
1968. Congressional Record, CXIV, 24945.
    Memorial to King by Kalvert D. Nelson of Oklahoma
City.

————. ————. ————. 91st Cong., 1st sess., January 15,
1969. Congressional Record, CXV, 866.
    Senator Brooke (Mass.) introduces a resolution to
make January 15 "Martin Luther King Day."

————. ————. ————. 91st Cong., 1st sess., January 15,
1969. Congressional Record, CXV, 909.
    Poetic tribute to King by Marguerite M. Marshall
and Antoinette Yolkum.

————. ————. House. 91st Cong., 1st sess., January 15,
1969. Congressional Record, CXV, 962.
    Representative Moorhead (Pa.) introduces legislation
to have a commemorative medal issued.

————. ————. ————. 91st Cong., 1st sess., January 23,
1969. Congressional Record, CXV, 1706.
    Representative Mikva (Ill.) introduces legislation to
make January 15 a national holiday.

————. ————. ————. 91st Cong., 1st sess., February 26,
1969. Congressional Record, CXV, 4536-37. (Also

found on p. 4644 and 4681.)

Remarks by Representative Conyers (Mich.) supporting legislation to make King's birthday [January 15] a public holiday.

————. ——. ——. 91st Cong. , 1st sess. , February 26, 1969. Congressional Record, CXV, 4540-41.

Representative Horton (N. Y.) comments on letters received from Rochester school children in memory of King.

————. ——. ——. 91st Cong. , 1st sess. , April 2, 1969. Congressional Record, CXV, 8473.

Memorial remarks by Representative Burton (Calif.).

————. ——. ——. 91st Cong. , 1st sess. , April 3, 1969. Congressional Record, CXV, 8557-58.

Memorial remarks by Representative Ryan (N. Y.).

————. ——. Senate. 91st Cong. , 1st sess. , April 3, 1969. Congressional Record, CXV, 8603-4.

Senator Griffin (Mich.) introduces legislation for the issuance of a commemorative stamp for King.

————. ——. ——. 91st Cong. , 1st sess. , April 3, 1969. Congressional Record, CXV, 8664-65.

Memorial remarks by Senator Goodell (N. Y.).

————. ——. ——. 91st Cong. , 1st sess. , April 3, 1969. Congressional Record, CXV, 8673.

Memorial remarks by Senator Bayh (Ind.).

————. ——. ——. 91st Cong. , 1st sess. , April 3, 1969. Congressional Record, CXV, 8675-76.

Memorial remarks by Senator Williams (N. J.).

————. ——. House. 91st Cong. , 1st sess. , April 3, 1969. Congressional Record, CXV, 8734.

Memorial remarks by Representative Diggs (Mich.).

————. ——. ——. 91st Cong. , 1st sess. , April 3, 1969. Congressional Record, CXV, 8734-35.

Text of Robert Kennedy's statement to an Indianapolis crowd upon learning of King's death.

————. ——. ——. 91st Cong. , 1st sess. , April 3, 1969. Congressional Record, CXV, 8737-38.

Memorial remarks by Representative Farbstein (N. Y.).

_____. _____. _____. 91st Cong. , 1st sess. , April 14, 1969. Congressional Record, CXV, 8932-33.
Remarks by Representative Nix (Pa.) supporting the issuance of a commemorative stamp.

_____. _____. _____. 91st Cong. , 1st sess. , April 18, 1969. Congressional Record, CXV, 9625-27.
Text of a memorial address delivered by Dr. John Hope Franklin.

_____. _____. _____. 91st Cong. , 1st sess. , June 2, 1969. Congressional Record, CXV, 14427-45.
Reprints of previous Cong. Record material by Representative Rarick (La.) alleging King's association with Communism.

_____. _____. _____. 91st Cong. , 1st sess. , June 5, 1969. Congressional Record, CXV, 14957-72.
Reprints of previous memorial statements made following King's death.

_____. _____. _____. 91st Cong. , 1st sess. , July 9, 1969. Congressional Record, CXV, 18817-18.
Address by Richard H. Mitchell of Richmond, Calif. , concerning King's death.

_____. _____. _____. 91st Cong. , 1st sess. , September 19, 1969. Congressional Record, CXV, 26424.
Reprint of radio editorial about King's death by station WVOX of New Rochelle, N. Y.

_____. _____. _____. 91st Cong. , 1st sess. , December 12, 1969. Congressional Record, CXV, 38955.
Text of a proclamation of tribute to King issued by Governor John Dempsey of Connecticut.

_____. _____. _____. 91st Cong. , 2nd sess. , January 20, 1970. Congressional Record, CXVI, 388.
Text of a resolution passed by the Kentucky State Senate supporting legislation to make King's birthday a public holiday.

_____. _____. _____. 91st Cong. , 2nd sess. , January 21, 1970. Congressional Record, CXVI, 615-16.
Remarks by Representative Ryan (N. Y.) supporting

the creation of a holiday on January 15.

_____. _____. _____. 91st Cong. , 2nd sess. , January 22,
1970. Congressional Record, CXVI, 879-80.
Representative Dulski (N. Y.) comments on tributes
to King in Buffalo.

_____. _____. _____. 91st Cong. , 2nd sess. , January 27,
1970. Congressional Record, CXVI, 1414.
Poetic memorial by Anthony Cama.

_____. _____. _____. 91st Cong. , 2nd sess. , January 28,
1970. Congressional Record, CXVI, 1593.
Text of a resolution passed by the Kentucky House
of Representatives supporting legislation to make King's
birthday a public holiday.

_____. _____. _____. 91st Cong. , 2nd sess. , March 3, 1970.
Congressional Record, CXVI, 5776-77.
Text of a resolution from Gary, Ind. , supporting
legislation to make King's birthday a national holiday.

_____. _____. _____. 91st Cong. , 2nd sess. , March 26, 1970.
Congressional Record, CXVI, 9518-20.
Remarks by Representative Heckler (Mass.) concerning the issuance of a medal to honor King; also a reprint of an Encounter article by Henry Fairlie.

_____. _____. Senate. 91st Cong. , 2nd sess. , March 26,
1970. Congressional Record, CXVI, 9548-49.
Comments by Senator Scott (Pa.) in support of the
issuance of a commemorative medal.

_____. _____. House. 91st Cong. , 2nd sess. , April 16, 1970.
Congressional Record, CXVI, 12290-91.
Reprint of article by George S. Schuyler, "Saint Mar-
tin?--The Martin Luther King Memorial. "

_____. _____. Senate. 91st Cong. , 2nd sess. , July 23, 1970.
Congressional Record, CXVI, 25696-99.
Remarks by Senator Tunney (Calif.) concerning the
All Star baseball game played as a tribute to King.

_____. _____. House. 91st Cong. , 2nd sess. , October 14,
1970. Congressional Record, CXVI, 36756-57. (Also
found on p. 33669-70.)
Remarks by Representative Bingham (N. Y.) support-

ing legislation to have a bust or statue of King placed in the Capitol.

_____.   .   ____.   91st Cong., 2nd sess., December 19, 1970. Congressional Record, CXVI, 42829-30.
Resolutions supporting a holiday on King's birthday issued by the University of Santa Clara (California) and the Jewish Community Council of San Jose, Calif.

_____.   ____.   Senate.   92nd Cong., 1st sess., January 25, 1971. Congressional Record, CXVII, 362.
Legislation to make January 15 a national day of commemoration is introduced by Senator Brooke (Mass.).

_____.   ____.   House.   92nd Cong., 1st sess., February 10, 1971. Congressional Record, CXVII, 2338-40.
Remarks by Representative Conyers (Mich.) and a list of other congressmen and governors supporting legislation to make King's birthday a national holiday.

_____.   ____.   Senate.   92nd Cong., 1st sess., February 10, 1971. Congressional Record, CXVII, 2468.
Senator McGovern (S. D.) introduces legislation to make King's birthday a national holiday.

_____.   ____.   House.   92nd Cong, 1st sess., April 1, 1971. Congressional Record, CXVII, 9033-34. (Also p. 2933-34, 10128-29.
Remarks by Representative Nix (Pa.) in support of the issuance of a commemorative stamp for King.

_____.   ____.   Senate.   92nd Cong., 1st sess., June 3, 1971. Congressional Record, CXVII, 17757-58.
Senator Humphrey (Minn.) introduces legislation to make King's birthplace a national historic site.

_____.   ____.   House.   92nd Cong., 1st sess., July 31, 1971. Congressional Record, CXVII, 28599-600. (Also p. 38324.)
Remarks by Representative Fauntroy (D. C.) in support of legislation to make King's birthday a holiday in the District of Columbia.

_____.   .   ____.   92nd Cong., 2nd sess., January 19, 1972. Congressional Record, CXVIII, 371.
Representative Ryan (N. Y.) supports legislation to make King's birthday a national holiday.

____. ____. Senate. 93rd Cong., 1st sess., January 12, 1973. Congressional Record, CXIX, 1039.
Remarks by Senator Humphrey (Minn.) honoring the 44th anniversary of King's birth.

____. ____. House. 93rd Cong., 1st sess., January 15, 1973. Congressional Record, CXIX, 1093.
Representative Madden (Ind.) honors the 44th anniversary of King's birth.

____. ____. ____. 93rd Cong., 1st sess., January 15, 1973. Congressional Record, CXIX, 1104-05.
Representative Anderson (Ill.) honors the 44th anniversary of King's birth.

____. ____. ____. 93rd Cong., 1st sess., January 15, 1973. Congressional Record, CXIX, 1111.
Representative Lehman (Fla.) honors the 44th anniversary of King's birth.

____. ____. Senate. 93rd Cong., 1st sess., January 16, 1973. Congressional Record, CXIX, 1132.
Senator Scott (Pa.) honors the 44th anniversary of King's birth.

____. ____. ____. 93rd Cong., 1st sess., January 16, 1973. Congressional Record, CXIX, 1197.
Text of Senate Joint Resolution 20, which would make January 15 a national holiday.

____. ____. House. 93rd Cong., 1st sess., January 18, 1973. Congressional Record, CXIX, 1619-24.
Representative Stokes (Ohio) in support of creating a national holiday to honor King.

____. ____. ____. 93rd Cong., 1st sess., January 20, 1973. Congressional Record, CXIX, 1670.
Representative Grasso (Conn.) pays tribute to King.

____. ____. ____. 93rd Cong., 1st sess., January 24, 1973. Congressional Record, CXIX, 2165.
Remarks by Representative Hudnut (Ind.) in support of legislation to make King's birthday a national holiday.

____. ____. ____. 93rd Cong., 1st sess., January 26, 1973. Congressional Record, CXIX, 2350.
Representative Burke (Calif.) pays tribute to King.

. . . 93rd Cong., 1st sess., January 26,
1973. Congressional Record, CXIX, 2358-59.
Representative Abzug (N. Y.) comments on a petition
received from some New York school children in support
of making King's birthday a national holiday.

. . . 93rd Cong., 1st sess., February 6,
1973. Congressional Record, CXIX, 3469.
Text of a resolution passed by the Colorado General
Assembly making January 15 a state holiday.

. . . 93rd Cong., 1st sess., February 7,
1973. Congressional Record, CXIX, 3887-88.
Representative Young (Ga.) comments on Atlanta's
tribute to King on the 44th anniversary of his birth.

. . . 93rd Cong., 1st sess., March 1, 1973.
Congressional Record, CXIX, 6051.
Remarks by Representative Rodino in support of
legislation to make King's birthday a holiday.

. . . 93rd Cong., 1st sess., March 15, 1973.
Congressional Record, CXIX, 8304.
Text of the song, "My Beloved," written by Rachel
Leon in memory of King and Robert Kennedy.

. . . 93rd Cong., 1st sess., April 4, 1973.
Congressional Record, CXIX, 11094.
Remarks by Representative Jordan (Texas) on the
fifth anniversary of King's assassination.

. . . 93rd Cong., 1st sess., April 4, 1973.
Congressional Record, CXIX, 11138.
Remarks by Representative Rangel (N. Y.) on the
fifth anniversary of King's assassination.

. . . 93rd Cong., 1st sess., April 5, 1973.
Congressional Record, CXIX, 11281.
Remarks by Representative Abzug (N. Y.) on the
fifth anniversary of King's assassination.

. . . 93rd Cong., 1st sess., April 16, 1973.
Congressional Record, CXIX, 12619.
Remarks by Representative Rodino (N. J.) concerning
the eighth annual Attucks-King memorial parade in New-
ark.

IV

REVIEWS OF BOOKS BY KING

STRIDE TOWARD FREEDOM

Ahmann, Matthew. Ave Maria, LXXXIII (November 22, 1958), p. 27-28.

Ascherson, Neal. "Alabama, Up We Come. " Spectator, CCII (May 15, 1959), p. 707.

Ashmore, Harry S. "Martin Luther King, Spokesman for the Southern Negro. " New York Herald Tribune Book Review (September 21, 1958), p. 5.

Booklist & Subscription Books Bulletin, LV (October 1, 1958), p. 60+.

Bookmark, XVIII (October, 1956), p. 8.

"Bus Boycott in Alabama. " Times Literary Supplement (September 18, 1959), p. 534.

Campbell, Ernest Q. Social Forces, XXXVIII (October, 1959), p. 74-77.

Henderson, Robert W. Library Journal, LXXXIII (October 1, 1958), p. 2751.

Hurley, Philip S. "The Montgomery Story. " Social Order, VIII (December, 1958), p. 485-86.

Isaacs, Harold R. "Civil Disobedience in Montgomery. " New Republic, CXXXIX (October 6, 1958), p. 19-20.

Lehman, W. Community, XVIII (January, 1959), p. 6.

Liggett, William. Interracial Review, XXXI (November, 1958), p. 199.

MacKenzie, Norman. "A Victory in Alabama. " New Statesman, LVII (June 6, 1959), p. 800.

Miller, Perry. "The Mind and Faith of Martin Luther King. " Reporter, XIX (October 30, 1958), p. 40.

New Yorker, XXXIV (September 20, 1958), p. 173+.

Plenn, Abel. "The Cradle Was Rocked. " New York Times Book Review, October 12, 1958, p. 24.

"Revolution and Redemption. " Christian Century, LXXV (September 24, 1958), p. 1070-1.

Schwenn, Roger. Wisconsin Library Bulletin, LIV (November-December, 1958), p. 510.

Smith, Lillian. "And Suddenly Something Happened. " Saturday Review, XLI (September 20, 1958), p. 21.

Virginia Kirkus Bulletin, XXVI (July 15, 1958), p. 533.

STRENGTH TO LOVE

Byam, Milton S. Library Journal, LXXXVIII (July, 1963), p. 2704.

Gasnick, Roy M. America, CIX (August 17, 1963), p. 173-74.

Lynd, Staughton. "The New Negro Radicalism. " Commentary, XXXVI (September, 1963), p. 252-56.

McNally, Arthur. Sign, XLIII (September, 1963), p. 61-62.

Marie, Sister Claire. "Reviewer Wants More Preachers Like This. " Community, XXIII (March, 1964), p. 13.

Sweazey, George E. Sermons of Substance. " Christian Century, LXXX (July 17, 1963), p. 911.

TRUMPET OF CONSCIENCE

Booklist & Subscription Books Bulletin, LXV (October 1, 1968), p. 134.

Publishers' Weekly, CXCIII (June 10, 1968), p. 60.

Virginia Kirkus Bulletin, XXXVI (June 15, 1968), p. 674.

Virginia Quarterly Review, XLIX (Autumn, 1968), p. 174.

WHERE DO WE GO FROM HERE: CHAOS OR COMMUNITY?

Booklist & Subscription Books Bulletin, XV (July 15, 1967), p. 1169.

Carter, M. B. Observer, March 24, 1968, p. 28.

Choice, IV (February, 1968), p. 117.

Drinan, R. F. America, CXVII (July 22, 1967), p. 88.

Duberman, Martin. Bookweek (July 9, 1967), p. 1.

Economist, CCXXVII (April 6, 1968), p. 51.

Goode, B. Antioch Review, XXVIII (Spring, 1968), p. 117.

Ions, E. New Statesman, LXXV (March 22, 1968), p. 384.

Konvitz, Milton R. Saturday Review, L (July 8, 1967), p. 29.

Kopkind, Andrew. New York Review of Books, IX (August 24, 1967), p. 3.

Kugler, R. F. Library Journal, XCII (June 15, 1967), p. 2426.

Luecke, Richard. Christian Century, LXXXIV (August 23, 1967), p. 1070.

Meier, August. Social Education, XXXII (February, 1968), p. 183.

158 / Martin Luther King, Jr.

"The Movement--2." Times Literary Supplement (April 18, 1968), p. 393-94.

New Yorker, XLIII (July 22, 1967), p. 88.

Publishers' Weekly, CXCI (April 24, 1967), p. 90.

Roberts, Gene. New York Times Book Review (September 3, 1967), p. 3.

Salkey, A. Punch, CCLIV (April 3, 1968), p. 501.

Seidenspinner, C. Books Today, IV (June 25, 1967), p. 6.

Steinberg, David. Commonweal, LXXXVII (November 17, 1967), p. 215.

Virginia Kirkus Bulletin, XXXV (April 15, 1967), p. 541.

WHY WE CAN'T WAIT

Agius, Ambrose. Best Sellers, XXIV (June 15, 1964), p. 123-24.

Boyd, Malcolm. Christian Century, LXXXI (August 26, 1964), p. 1064-65.

Brooks, Jerome. Sign, XLIV (August, 1964), p. 60-61.

Byam, Milton S. Library Journal, LXXXIX (June 1, 1964), p. 2359. (Also November 15, 1964, p. 4661.)

Clark, Dennis. "Toward Equality." Commonweal, LXXX (July 24, 1964), p. 518-19.

Donovan, J. B. Bookweek (June 7, 1964), p. 5.

Fuller, H. Negro Digest, XIV (February, 1965), p. 53.

McNaspy, C. J. "Reading for a Hot Summer." America, CX (June 20, 1964), p. 851-52.

Newsweek, LXIV (December 21, 1964), p. 83.

Redding, Saunders. "To Lift the Siege of Denial." New York Times Book Review (July 26, 1964), p. 1+.

Scoggin, M. C. Horn Book, XL (October, 1964), p. 516.

Stone, C. Sumner. "With Urgent Eloquence." Critic, XXIII (August-September, 1964), p. 76-77.

Times Literary Supplement (October 8, 1964), p. 915.

AUTHOR INDEX
(Coauthors, Editors, Compilers)

Abernathy, Ralph D.   94
Adams, Russell L.   71
Adler, Renata   94
Adoff, Arnold   14
Agius, Ambrose   158
Ahmann, Matthew   14, 155
Alabama State College   68
Alexander, Mithrapuram   27
Allen, Harold C.   71
Allen, R. R.   19
Allen, Robert L.   71
Altman, Dennis P.   94
Alvarez, Joseph A.   71
American Civil Liberties
  Union   69
Ames, William C.   14
Anatol, Karl W.   95
Andrews, James R.   15
Archer, F. M.   55
Arlen, Michael J.   95
Ascherson, Neal   155
Ashmore, Harry S.   155
Atkinson, Carolyn O.   96
Auer, Bernard M.   96
Austin, Aleine   96

Baker, Ross K.   15
Baldwin, James   27, 96
Bales, James D.   27, 34
Balfour, Nancy   96
Balk, Alfred   34
Banks, James A.   71
Banyai, Ed   96
Barrett, Catherine O'C.   34
Barrett, George   96
Bartlett, Robert M.   72

Beardwood, Roger   96
Belafonte, Harry   34
Bell, Derrick A.   15
Bell, Inge P.   72
Benedetti, Robert R.   142
Bennett, John C.   34
Bennett, Lerone, Jr.   27, 34,
  72, 97
Bergman, Peter M.   72
Berry, Mary F.   72
Bims, Hamilton   98
Birnie, Ian H.   72
Bishop, Jim   27
Bittner, John R.   95
Black, Edwin   73
Blackwelder, Julia K.   142
Blaustein, Albert P.   15
Bleeckey, Ted   98
Bleiweiss, Robert M.   27
Blumberg, Herbert H.   18
Boeth, Richard   98
Boggs, James   73
Booker, Simeon   35, 73, 99
Boone-Jones, Margaret   28
Bosmajian, Haig A.   15, 35
Bosmajian, Hamida   15
Bottone, Sam   99
Boulware, Marcus H.   15
Boutelle, Paul   73
Bowles, Chester   99
Boyd, Malcolm   73, 158
Boyle, Sarah P.   1, 99
Bracey, John H.   15, 73
Braden, Anne   99
Branson, Margaret S.   15
Breitman, George   99
Brennecke, Harry E.   35

161